Transnational Business Collaboration Among Common Market Countries

PRAEGER SPECIAL STUDIES IN
INTERNATIONAL ECONOMICS AND DEVELOPMENT

Transnational Business Collaboration Among Common Market Countries

ITS IMPLICATION FOR POLITICAL INTEGRATION

Werner J. Feld

Foreword by
J. Robert Schaetzel

PRAEGER PUBLISHERS
New York · Washington · London

The purpose of Praeger Special Studies is to make specialized research in U.S. and international economics and politics available to the academic, business, and government communities. For further information, write to the Special Projects Division, Praeger Publishers, Inc., 111 Fourth Avenue, New York, N.Y. 10003.

PRAEGER PUBLISHERS
111 Fourth Avenue, New York, N.Y. 10003, U.S.A.
5, Cromwell Place, London S.W.7, England

Published in the United States of America in 1970
by Praeger Publishers, Inc.

Library of Congress Catalog Card Number: 78-131947

Printed in the United States of America

FOREWORD

The European Communities are stirring after a long period
of relative stagnation. Today there is a strong sense of forward
movement which has not been present since the early 1960's
and a belief that further progress on several important fronts
can be made within the Community framework. A number of
developments over the past year have contributed to this favorable atmosphere: The Hague Summit Meeting in December
1969; the end of the Common Market's transitional period; the
beginning of serious discussions on economic and monetary
union; the naming of a new nine-man Commission; and the opening of negotiations with the United Kingdom, Ireland, Denmark,
and Norway for membership in the Community.

As Professor Feld points out in his preface, the inspira-
tion for his study of transnational business collaboration in
Europe came from an earlier period--a time, as he puts it, of
"abject stagnation" following the 1965 crisis. Searching for a
"catalyst which might move political integration forward again, "
he decided to examine the role of the business executives in
member states of the Community who are engaged in various
forms of cooperation with firms in other member states.

His study, however, is just as relevant to the present as
it is to the period before The Hague Summit. Atmosphere alone
is not an adequate measure of European political integration.
In fact, at any given time, scholars and other outside observers,
as well as the participants in the integration process itself, are
apt to disagree widely over whether political integration is moving forward rapidly or slowly, or even whether it is moving
forward at all. The difficulty of measurement arises from the
great complexity of the process. Political integration involves
not only such factors as the transfer of powers and responsibilities from the national governments to the Community institutions, or the creation of a new body of law by the Community's
Court of Justice but also a wide range of activities in the private sector, as well as more intangible, psychological factors.
Accurate assessments depend on as complete an understanding
of the many elements of the process as possible. In "The
European Common Market and the World, " Professor Feld
made an important contribution to our understanding of one
element: the transfer of responsibility for some aspects of

the conduct of foreign relations from the member state governments to the Community institutions. Now he has analyzed
another key element: transnational business collaboration.

Professor Feld examines the growth of this collaboration
over the past decade, its motiviations and objectives, and the
problems it has encountered. He examines both intrinsic prob-
lems--cultural differences and divergences· in methods and
goals--and problems caused by factors outside the collaborativ
process.

His conclusions are realistic. He finds that transnational
business collaboration has produced more economic integration
but its effect on political integration has been slight up to now.
Nevertheless he considers that the continuing growth of this
collaboration should, in time, lead to further advances in political integration. The executives of some of the firms he
has studied--especially the younger executives--have developed
a feeling of belonging to a "European" group, with shared value
and expectations. And, for economic reasons, the businessme
participating in transnational ventures have been pressing for
objectives such as the harmonization of fiscal laws and laws
setting technical standards, the creation of a "European company" statute, and the closer coordination of economic and
monetary policies, which would have the effect of increasing
the authority of the Community institutions.

In developing his analysis, Professor Feld finds that Britis
firms participate as actively in the process of transnational col
laboration in the EEC as firms based in the member states,
and discusses the implications of this participation for the enlargement of the Communities. He also examines the effect
of the "American challenge" on the process and describes the
important memorandum on industrial policy which the European
Commission sent to the member states earlier this year. Professor Feld sums up with an interesting discussion of the implications of his findings for integration theory and, in particul
for the continued validity of the "spill over" process.

Transnational business collaboration in Europe is not a
subject that is well-documented in sources that are readily
available to the public. This study is based on extensive interviews with business executives, leaders of interest groups and
political parties, and officials of national governments and of
the Commission of the European Communities. Professor Feld
has performed a valuable service by collecting original data
on this elusive, but timely subject. His analysis of the data
will benefit the observers of European affairs who want to get

behind the atmospherics to the underlying forces that are con-
tributing to the process of political integration.

J. Robert Schaetzel

United States Representative
to the European Communities

PREFACE

The idea of this book was born when the European Economic Community (EEC), or Common Market, found itself in a period of abject stagnation following the 1965 crisis provoked by President Charles de Gaulle, whose intent was to emasculate whatever progress had been made in the realm of political integration. In the search for a catalyst that might move political integration forward again, it seemed to me that the increasing interest of business management in border-crossing collaboration with similar firms in the Common Market might arouse the needed stimulus for such a movement. The basic questions that came to mind were the following: What influence would the businessman have in propelling the Common Market toward greater political integration? Which role could he play in garnering support among politically powerful elites for these plans and objectives? What would be the specific implications of a spreading net of border-crossing business collaboration for the process of integration? What were the techniques used for transnational business ventures and which factors would favor their success or impede their realization and smooth functioning?

Following President de Gaulle's retirement from the active political leadership of France and President Georges Pompidou's more favorable orientation toward full implementation of the Common Market treaty, a new invigoration of the spirit of Europe became evident. The summit meeting at The Hague in December, 1969, attended by the heads of state and chiefs of government of the EEC member states, produced new plans and programs to revive the life of the European Community (i.e., the European Atomic Energy Community, the European Coal and Steel Community, and the European Economic Community) after the stagnation of the preceding five years and to achieve the objectives set by the Common Market treaty. But announcements of change and new plans tend to reflect the intentions of political leaders; the realistic prospects of implementing these plans and intentions may not be as bright as the rhetoric leads one to believe. Implementation is likely to depend on the goals, expectations, and attitudes of powerful elites, some of whom might be at least, reluctant to carry out these plans--if they are not, in fact, strongly opposed to them. This work will explore these forces, not only as they affect the fortunes of transnational business collaboration but also with respect to the general implications for the progress of political integration in the European Community.

This study would have been impossible without the active cooperation of a score of business executives, government officials, political-party leaders, and interest-group officials in the member states of the European Community. In addition, valuable help was received from various functionaries of the European Community. To all of them I owe a tremendous debt of gratitude. While it would be impossible to mention the names of all these individuals, a few of them rendered particularly valuable service: Umberto Agnelli, Hans Beekhuis, Louis Joly, Dr. H. le Page, Arno Muenchwander, Gottfried Noack, and Jean-Claude Roussel. My most sincere thanks also go to Mrs. Donald Davis, who typed innumerable drafts of this manuscript without a murmur of complaint and willingly devoted time beyond the call of duty to this project.

Finally, I should like to acknowledge the financial assistance of the Ford Foundation and the American Philosophical Society for the conduct of field research without which this volume could not have been written.

None of the individuals named above is responsible for any errors of commission or ommission, for which I bear full responsibility.

CONTENTS

Chapter	Page

LIST OF TABLES

Transnational Business Collaboration Among Common Market Countries

CHAPTER 1   CONCEPTS AND SCOPE

One of the most intriguing aspects of contemporary international politics is the growing incidence of nongovernmental actors whose activities have an impact on the international system. Although national governments seek to exercise exclusive control over their external relations, nongovernmental organizations play an expanding role. Among the latter are not only traditional organizations, such as the International Chamber of Commerce, the League of Red Cross Societies, and many others pursuing a wide range of objectives, but also, increasingly, entities in the private business sector--in particular, multinational corporations and enterprises engaged in transnational collaboration in various forms. (Some observers believe that the world's economy of the future will be dominated by 300-400 giant multinational corporations.) The potential magnitude of the impact on the international system and its subsystems by these enterprises becomes evident when one considers that the transnational operations may involve capital investments, market development, or the exploitation of technological advance, which, in turn, may bring about pressures on local wages, industrial overcapacities, changes in the balance-of-payments, and other desirable and undesirable consequences in one or several countries.

Transnational business collaboration is a phenomenon that can be observed in many parts of the world. But it is apt to be especially significant among firms of countries that are pursuing a regional economic integration scheme, as is the case in the European Common Market, technically the European Economic Community (EEC), or the Latin American Free Trade Association (LAFTA). If, under these circumstances, a substantial number of enterprises in two or more countries should be involved in border-crossing collaboration, the resulting widespread pattern of interlacement may well have definitive effects upon the economic structures of the countries in the area, either in particular sectors or as a whole. In addition, it could give rise to a variety of political consequences

3

and conceivably contribute to a gradual transformation of the existing political structures in the regional international subsystem.

It is indeed among the member countries of the EEC that a rising trend of transnational business collaboration has become manifest since 1960.[1] Both very large enterprises and smaller firms have engaged in joint ventures. This is perhaps not surprising when one considers that the customs union upon which the EEC is predicated has been implemented ahead of the twelve-year schedule and the free movement of labor and business establishments is now being assured to an increasing degree. Transnational business collaboration ventures, therefore, can benefit from an expanded internal market, make use of the economies of scale whenever this should prove to be advantageous, and optimalize the allocation of resources.

The purpose of this study is to examine both the reasons for the expansion of transnational business collaboration among enterprises in the Common Market countries and the problems encountered by firms contemplating or engaged in this activity. A major part of this inquiry will be devoted to the political aspects of transnational collaboration within the EEC and, specifically, to the implications that this activity may have for the process of political integration in the Common Market.[2]

NATURE OF TRANSNATIONAL
BUSINESS COLLABORATION

As understood in this book, transnational business collaboration refers to long-term collaborative endeavors across national borders by two or more economic entities located in different countries of the EEC. It goes beyond a mere export and import trade relationship under which orders are placed with different suppliers according to the most favorable terms available. Rather, it aims at partnership in a broad sense--ideally with a well-defined common interest--and suggests a border-crossing interlacement of efforts on the part of the entities involved in the collaboration.

This interlacement must not be understood merely in terms of technical contributions to the cooperative efforts by the participating units and their staffs. As Wolfgang G. Friedmann points out in his study of joint international business ventures, there is also an emotive side to such efforts, which produces in the staff members and operating personnel

directly concerned with the collaboration a distinct feeling of
being involved in a "united or cooperative" endeavor.[3] This
is an important dimension of transnational business collaboration because it points to the border-crossing human and social
relations created by the collaboration schemes in addition to
economic and administrative transactional flows.

Since the major concern of this work is the political aspects of transnational business collaboration in the national
and international spheres, such terms as "partnership" and
"joint ventures" will be used in a broad, nontechnical sense.
In general, these terms are understood to refer to organizational structures under which the top management is divided
among several units, each located in a different country. The
tie between the units may be a collaboration agreement that
leaves the corporate structures of the participating firms untouched and excludes any investment schemes among the
partners. A more intense collaboration is likely to be established when the agreement includes the investment by one of
the participating firms in the enterprise of the other. In the
latter case, the undertaking may be called an "equity" joint
venture, while, in the former case, it is a "nonequity" joint
venture.[4] Under some collaboration agreements new corporate
structures may be created, either in the form of a holding
company, a jointly owned subsidiary, or, in fact, two corporations, as in the case of Agfa-Gevaerts. (See pp. 38-39,
below.) In all these cases top management is distributed,
though perhaps unevenly, among two or more headquarters
located in different countries and the collaboration venture
functions more or less like an international coalition.

The conditions differ, however, when it comes to wholly
owned subsidiaries whose parent company is situated in
another country. Then, the terms "partnership" and "joint
venture" may well be inappropriate, since top management
control is usually vested in the parent company and a command
hierarchy exists. Nevertheless, since it is the border-
crossing flow of human, social, administrative, and economic
relations and transactions between the two entities and their
consequent interlacement that have particular relevance for
this study, the inclusion of wholly owned subsidiaries under
these terms seems warranted. Similar considerations also
apply to transnational mergers or acquisitions that may lead
to the creation of a new corporation or changes in an existing
one.

How do multinational corporations fit into transnational
collaboration schemes? As defined by Raymond Vernon, these

corporations are "a cluster of corporations of diverse nationality joined together by ties of common ownership and re-
sponsive to a common management strategy. "[5] They operate,
therefore, in the different countries basically as national companies, a fact that is often politically very significant, for
example, when it comes to defense orders, which national
governments in most cases prefer to bestow upon national
enterprises. In terms of top management, some of the multinational corporations, such as Unilever and Royal Dutch-Shell,
pursue a polycentric pattern under which management has been
established for each zone. Obviously, a substantial flow of
transnational interaction is necessary to coordinate the management activities of the separate base companies. But even
if the top management is organized in a monocentric manner,
with one base company functioning as the management organ
for all international operations, significant transnational flows
between subordinate administrative units take place, suggest-
ing that the notion of partnership in a broad sense is applicable
in those cases as well. [6]

Moreover, multinational corporations can also engage
operationally in border-crossing activities; an illustration
would be the rationalization of production by using the best-
suited manufacturing facilities in different EEC countries for
a particular product. Opel, the General Motors German
affiliate, builds and assembles the body of one of its models
in France, while its mechanical parts come from Opel's West
German factory. Philips is also beginning to do this in the
production of radio sets. Since this process involves closing
production lines in one EEC country and using longer production runs in another, it is a politically sensitive undertaking
requiring careful balancing of activities in the countries involved.

ORGANIZATION AND SCOPE

This study is organized into four major sections. Chapter
1 provides a brief general setting and overview of the subject.
Chapter 2 contains an examination of the growth, motivations,
and objectives of transnational business collaboration among
the Common Market countries, as well as a discussion of the
methods and techniques used for the collaboration ventures.
The various problems encountered in the management of these
ventures are also analyzed.

Chapter 3 treats the political sphere. It begins with an
investigation of the principal objectives pursued by the collaborating entities--namely, those requiring favorable action
by the national authorities of the EEC member states of the
European Community institutions. (The European Community
refers collectively to the European Atomic Energy Community,
the European Coal and Steel Community, and the European
Economic Community.) It then goes into an examination of
the tactics and means employed for the attainment of these
objectives and seeks to evaluate their effectiveness. In this
connection it is important to point out that, as the operations
of a company transcend the national setting, going beyond
mere export and import trade, the environmental framework
changes in many respects. New ground rules for management
and operations arise from laws, cultures, and customs prevailing in the countries of the collaborating firms. New opportunities spring up, but new uncertainties also burden managerial
decision-making. The government of the country into which an
enterprise may want to extend its activities might seek to place
constraints on the scope of these activities. The possibility
that the objectives of the enterprise might be at variance with
the expressed national goals of the host government compound
this problem. [7]

The last part of Chapter 3 consists of an assessment of
the effect that transnational business collaboration within the
Common Market might have on the process of political integration. The role played by the continuing border-crossing
flow of administrative, technical, social, and human inter-
actions engendered by such collaboration among the personnel
of the enterprises involved is appraised. In addition, the
nature of the responses that politically influential actors in the
EEC member states are prepared to give to the demands of
companies engaged in border-crossing collaboration are
evaluated in terms of present perspective and the foreseeable
future.

Chapter 4 concludes this study with a brief examination
of the potential effect of the threat of the "American challenge"
on the role of transnational business collaboration in the Common Market as far as political integration is concerned. A
very tentative appraisal is made of the influence that extensive
transnational collaboration between British companies and
firms located inside the Common Market might have on the
prospect of membership for Britain. Finally, the new insights
into political integration theory that have emerged from this
study are analyzed, especially regarding whether and under

what conditions economic integration in an international region
such as the European Community automatically engenders
political integration.

In view of the scope of this study, it is immaterial whether
control or ownership either of enterprises engaged in intra-
EEC transnational collaboration or of the parent company of
a subsidiary situated in another EEC country is in the hands of
firms whose main corporate base and "home office" are located outside the Common Market. The salient point is that
the collaboration takes place among entities in different Common Market countries.

CONCEPTUAL FRAMEWORK

Since this study is greatly concerned with the political
implications of transnational business collaboration in the
Common Market, it is only natural that its conceptual framework derive from the discipline of political science. In view
of the intense multilevel interaction in evolving decisions and
policies affecting Common Market activities among EEC institutions, the national authorities of the member states,
interest groups, and to a lesser extent political parties, it
seems advisable to adopt a framework that perceives the
political process in the Common Market in an inclusive fashion
An acceptable framework is provided by Leon Lindberg's concept of the EEC as an incipient political system in which the
member states are seen as subsystems whose authorities play
influential roles in the decision-making process of the system
as a whole.[8] Lindberg's concepts are based on work done by
David Easton regarding the nature of the political system.[9]

Easton defines the political system as that system of in-
teractions in any society (including prenational or multinational
societies) through which binding or authoritative allocations
of values are made and implemented. In such a system, transnational business collaboration ventures contribute to the input
into the decision-making machinery by articulating demands
to be made on pertinent national or central system authorities
and by offering support either to specific actions taken by the
system decision-makers or in general to the system values,
norms of conduct, and structures. The collaboration entities
will also be affected by the output of the system, which consists mainly of decisions and policies. The feedback from
this output may, in turn, stimulate new demands on the system,
generate new supports, or reinforce existing supports.

In view of the interest of this work in the relationship between transnational business collaboration and the process of integration, the latter term also requires definition. As conceived in this study, political integration is defined as a process whereby states forgo the desire and ability to conduct foreign and key domestic policies independently and instead seek to make joint decisions or delegate the decision-making process to new central organs. In addition, political actors are persuaded to shift their loyalties, expectations, and political activities to the new center.[10] Since political integration may well depend on how much progress has been made in the field of economic integration in a particular international region, the concept of the latter used here also needs to be made explicit. Following Bela Balassa, this process "encompasses measures designed to abolish discrimination between economic units belonging to different national states."[11] In addition, as Jan Tinbergen suggests, integration aims at the optimum operation of the unified economy as the artificial hindrances are removed and desirable elements of coordination and unification are introduced.[12]

SOURCES OF DATA

The empirical data presented in this study stem in part from fifty in-depth interviews and conversations with executives of firms engaged in transnational ventures in the Common market countries, with leaders of interest groups and political parties, and with officials of national administrations of the member states and the EEC Commission. Additional sources include financial and other reports made to stockholders by enterprises involved in border-crossing collaboration; the proceedings of conferences, held mainly in Europe, which addressed themselves directly or indirectly to problems of collaboration and industrial concentrations; and a variety of published and unpublished analyses and treatises bearing on the subject.

EXPANSION OF KNOWLEDGE

Although this inquiry concentrates on a relatively small sector of transnational business activity in a geographically restricted area, it may make a contribution to the study of the changing patterns of national-international linkages and their impact upon the persistence or transformation of international subsystems such as the EEC. If transformation were to result, it could, in turn, have ramifications for the international system as a whole. An equally important by-product of this work may be a better understanding of the impact that nongovernmental transnational forces, especially big business and perhaps also labor, have on both the national and international systems in which they are operating.[13]

NOTES

1.   LAFTA has also sought to stimulate consciously transnational collaboration among member-country industrial enterprises by the use of so-called complementarity agreements; however, the success of efforts in that direction has been very limited. See Sidney Dell, A Latin American Common Market? (New York: Oxford University Press, 1966), pp. 120-45.

2.   See the interesting article by Robert Lecourt, "Concentrations et fusions d'entreprises, facteurs d'intégration européenne," Revue du Marché Commun, No. 109 (January-February, 1968), pp. 6-24.

3.   Wolfgang G. Friedmann and George Kalmanoff, Joint International Business Ventures (New York: Columbia University Press, 1961), pp. 5-6. The two authors have focused their study mainly on joint ventures in developing countries with the partnerships organized between firms from advanced countries and local enterprises. However, some of the principles evolved by Friedmann and Kalmanoff are also applicable to joint ventures and other forms of transnational collaboration in developed countries.

4.   Endel J. Kolde, International Business Enterprise (Englewood Cliffs, N.J.: Prentice-Hall, 1968), p. 260. If capital is needed for a joint venture, it is raised from whichever capital market provides the best source for a particular undertaking. See also Kolde's discussion of the "transnational" company on p. 251.

5.   Raymond Vernon, "Economic Sovereignty at Bay," Foreign Affairs, XLVII, 1 (October, 1968), 114.

6.   See Kolde, op. cit., pp. 250-51.

7.   See Raymond Vernon, "Multinational Enterprise and National Sovereignty," Harvard Business Review (March-April, 1967), pp. 156-72, and Jack N. Behrman, "Multinational Corporations, Transnational Interests and National Sovereignty," Columbia Journal of World Business, IV, 2 (March-April, 1969), 15-21. Sometimes, the management of an enterprise may go so far as to plot with the opposition on the overthrow of a government. It may rationalize such action by taking the position that companies tend to take a longer-run view of national interests than some governments do, since the latter may be in office only a few years, while the company must stand on its behavior record over a long period of time. Of course, if it happens that the current government is sympathetic with the company's objectives, while the opposition frowns on the activities of the company, it may find the going quite difficult in the event that the opposition should win out. In fact, it may also be thrown out or eventually be compelled to pull up stakes.

8.   Leon N. Lindberg, "The European Community as a Political System: Notes Toward the Construction of a Model," Journal of Common Market Studies, V, 4 (June, 1967), 344-87.

9.   David Easton, A System Analysis of Political Life (New York: John Wiley and Sons, 1965).

10.   See Leon N. Lindberg, The Political Dynamics of European Economic Integration (Stanford, Calif.: Stanford University Press, 1963), p. 3, and Ernst B. Haas, The Uniting of Europe (Stanford, Calif.: Stanford University Press, 1968), p. 16.

11.   Bela Belassa, The Theory of Economic Integration (Homewood, Ill.: Richard D. Irwin, 1961), p. 1.

12.   Jan Tinbergen, International Economic Integration (2d rev. ed.; Amsterdam: Elsevier, 1965), p. 57.

13.   This remains a largely unexplored field in which much research is needed to gain more understanding of these new forces in international politics. For an interesting contribution, see Karl Kaiser, "Transnationale Politik," Politische Vierteljahresschrift, Special Issue, X, 1 (1969), 80-109. See also James N. Rosenau "Toward the Study of National-International Linkages," in James N. Rosenau, ed., Linkage Politics (New York: The Free Press, 1969), pp. 44-66.

CHAPTER **2** ECONOMIC FACTORS AND
MANAGEMENT

INCREASE IN COLLABORATION VENTURES

The statistics for measuring the growth and scope of
transnational collaboration in the Common Market are less
than satisfactory because the data currently available do not
cover the full range of joint ventures nor the size of the entities involved, especially their sales records, capitalization,
and employees. Only when rather large enterprises are participants in transnational ventures--and quite a few of Europe's
large corporations indeed are--can the latter information be
found periodically with relative ease. [1]

Nevertheless, the statistics available are at least suggestive, and the information presented in Table 1, which
covers collaboration ventures involving financial participations
and the establishment of subsidiaries, indicates a definite
upward trend of border-crossing endeavors, with 1968 being
a banner year. The full implementation of the customs union
on July 1 of that year may well have been the reason for the
remarkable increase in collaboration ventures, since for
many enterprises this may have been the signpost that the
movement toward full economic integration had passed the
point of no return. Preliminary and very tentative figures
indicate that the upward trend of transnational business collaboration has continued in 1969, although the increase was
less dramatic than it was in 1968. [2]

Over the years, however, there have been failures of
joint ventures, and some wholly owned subsidiaries may have
been abandoned. The reasons will be discussed below. (See
pp. 40-50.) Although these failures have motivated some firms
to opt for national collaborations, it is evident that others have
not been discouraged from engaging in new transnational endeavors.

TABLE 1

Transnational Collaboration Ventures
in EEC, 1959-68[a]

1959	1960	1961	1962	1963	1964	1965	1966	1967	1968	Total
24	30	71	68	93	121	151	138	164	565	1,425

[a]Includes financial participations, as well as wholly and jointly owned subsidiaries.

Sources: Robert Saclé, Revue du Marché Commun, No. 109 (January-February, 1968), p. 116; A. P. Weber, "Les mouvements de concentration en Europe et la pénétration industrielle et commerciale," Direction, No. 148 (March, 1968), pp. 262 ff.; and A. P. Weber, "Concentrations en Europe," Direction, No. 160 (April, 1969), pp. 392 ff.

PATTERN OF GEOGRAPHIC DISTRIBUTION

The national distribution of newly established marketing and production subsidiaries, as well as financial participations, within the EEC during 1967 and 1968 is shown in Tables 2 and 3. For comparison purposes, British and American transnational activities in the Common Market have also been included.

The distribution of marketing subsidiaries during both years suggests a strong German interest in the French market and a strong French interest in the German and Belgian/ Luxembourg markets. The Italians show a predilection for the French market during both years, whereas the Dutch have shifted from a major interest in the French and Belgian/ Luxembourg markets in 1967 to a predominant concern with the German market in 1968.

A somewhat different picture is revealed by the distribution of wholly and jointly owned production subsidiaries and financial participations. The German enterprises show a strong interest toward the French industrial complex, whereas

TABLE 2

Total of Marketing Subsidiaries Established
During 1967 and 1968 Within EEC[a]

Receiving Country	Originating Country Within EEC												Originating Country Outside EEC			
	Germany		France		Italy		Netherlands		Belgium/ Luxembourg		Total		Great Britain		U.S.A.	
	1967	1968	1967	1968	1967	1968	1967	1968	1967	1968	1967	1968	1967	1968	1967	1968
Germany	--	--	16	43	3	6	4	48	5	13	28	110	2	23	26	60
France	10	47	--	--	6	30	8	13	4	2	28	92	7	18	30	47
Italy	14	20	3	11	--	--	3	5	1	2	21	38	4	14	15	32
Netherlands	4	23	2	4	0	7	--	--	1	3	7	37	8	13	10	21
Belgium/ Luxembourg	6	20	5	31	2	5	7	30	--	--	20	86	6	16	22	46
Total	34	110	26	89	11	48	22	96	11	20	104	363	27	84	103	206

[a]Includes service organizations for 1968.

Sources: A. P. Weber, "Les Mouvements de concentration en Europe et la pénétration industrièlle et commerciale," Direction, No. 148 (March, 1968), p. 264; and A. P. Weber, "Concentrations en Europe," Direction, No. 160 (April, 1969), p. 393.

14

TABLE 3

Total of Production Subsidiaries and Financial Participations
Established During 1967 and 1968 Within EEC[a]

| Receiving Country | Originating Country Within EEC | | | | | | | | | | | | Originating Country Outside EEC | | | |
| | Germany | | France | | Italy | | Netherlands | | Belgium/ Luxembourg | | Total | | Great Britain | | U.S.A. | |
	1967	1968	1967	1968	1967	1968	1967	1968	1967	1968	1967	1968	1967	1968	1967	1968
Germany	--	--	1	4	0	0	3	12	1	4	5	20	10	14	29	53
France	11	40	--	--	2	12	3	8	5	9	21	69	6	30	34	54
Italy	2	5	5	14	--	--	1	0	0	4	8	23	3	18	25	31
Netherlands	3	11	2	3	0	0	--	--	0	6	5	20	3	20	19	39
Belgium/ Luxembourg	2	20	7	24	2	8	10	18	--	--	21	70	7	39	34	39
Total	18	76	15	45	4	20	17	38	6	23	60	202	29	121	141	216

aIncludes holding companies for 1968.

Sources: A. P. Weber, "Les Mouvements de concentration en Europe et la pénétration industrielle et commerciale," Direction, No. 148 (March, 1968), p. 264; and A. P. Weber, "Concentrations en Europe," Direction, No. 160 (April, 1969), p. 394.

French industry is drawn mainly toward Italy and Belgium/
Luxembourg. Italy, in turn, is interested only to a limited
extent in expanding its industrial orbit and, for this, prefers
France and the Belgium/Luxembourg area. The Dutch seek
some industrial penetration in all EEC countries except Italy,
where their interest is minimal.

In view of Great Britain's application for full EEC member
ship, it is noteworthy that the figure for British marketing sub
sidiaries in the Common Market compares favorably with those
of Germany, France, and the Netherlands and is substantially
higher than those of Italy and Belgium/Luxembourg. As for
production subsidiaries and financial participations, British
enterprises showed a considerably higher number of initiatives
in the EEC than did any of the member states. The 1968
figure for these British initiatives was the same as the combined total for Germany and France and was six times as high
as that of Italy. In 1967 the preferred EEC countries for
British market subsidiaries were, in order, the Netherlands,
France, and Belgium/Luxembourg and, for production units
and financial participations, Germany, Belgium/Luxembourg,
and France. In 1968 the preferred EEC countries for the
former category were, in order, Germany, France, and
Belgium/Luxembourg and, for the latter category, Belgium/
Luxembourg, France, and the Netherlands. The implications
of this relatively high level of transnational collaboration will
be discussed in the concluding chapter of this book.

The percentage increase in the establishment of U.S. subsidiaries in the Common Market and of financial participations
by American firms in EEC enterprises between 1967 and 1968
has been substantially smaller (173 per cent) than that of
EEC-based and British companies (344 and 366 per cent, respectively). In 1968, for the first time, the number of U.S.
ventures (422) fell below the intra-EEC figure (565); however,
it should be noted that these figures merely record the number
of joint ventures without saying anything about their size and
scope.

In 1967 and 1968 the preferred EEC countries for all U.S.
subsidiaries and financial participations were France, Germany, and Belgium/Luxembourg, although the order of rank
has shifted slightly from category to category and year to
year. It is noteworthy that plant and equipment expenditures
by Common Market affiliates of U.S. corporations dropped
from $1,437 million in 1967 to $1,194 million in 1968, but
increased again in 1969 to an estimated $1,584 million.[3]

DISTRIBUTION BY INDUSTRIES

The distribution of collaboration ventures among different sectors of the economy in the Common Market is shown in Tables 4 and 5. Table 4 is based on the total number of ventures for 1959-66, as presented in Table 1, and breaks this figure down into financial participations and wholly and jointly owned subsidiaries for various industries. Clearly, the chemical and oil industry was most heavily engaged in transnational collaboration ventures of various kinds, followed by the food-processing industry, the mechanical-engineering and automobile industry, and the electrical and electronics industry. Separate figures for the automobile industry indicate only a small number of ventures: five financial participations, nine wholly owned subsidiaries, and eleven jointly owned subsidiaries;[4] but, automobile manufacturing plants tend to be medium sized to large, and therefore the small number is a deceiving measure when assessing their contribution to the consequences of transnational collaboration.

Table 5 provides somewhat different information about collaboration ventures in 1968 inasmuch as it shows their distribution by economic sector and by the individual EEC countries that initiated the ventures. In 1968, the mechanical-engineering and automobile industry was involved in the greatest number of such ventures, followed closely by the chemical industry and with greater distances by the electrical and electronics industry and the textile and shoe industry.[5] A study conducted in 1968 by the Comité Européen pour le Progrès Economique et Social (CEPES)--a survey of 1,448 cases of transnational business collaboration in Western Europe, with primary emphasis on the Common Market, that included agreements without financial participations but excluded wholly owned subsidiaries--confirmed the pattern of industrial distribution indicated in Tables 4 and 5.[6] It should not be surprising that the chemical and electronics industries are in the forefront of the collaboration ventures, since the extremely high research expenditures necessary for these industries may be reduced through shared research. In the mechanical-engineering and automobile industry, the possibility of lower development and production costs through a division of labor and concentration on certain products makes collaboration agreements especially attractive.

Table 5 reveals the dynamics of German transnational initiatives, not only in the leading sectors identified above,

TABLE 4

Transnational Collaboration Ventures in EEC
According to Industrial Sectors, 1959-66

Sector	Financial Participations	Wholly Owned Subsidiaries	Jointly Owned Subsidiaries	Total
Food processing	14	50	41	105
Chemical & oil	40	66	88	194
Electrical & electronics	19	26	32	77
Mechanical engineering & automobile	8	45	49	102
Paper	6	3	1	10
Construction & construction materials	19	9	22	50
Textiles & shoes	17	31	22	70
Metallurgy	10	9	11	30
Miscellaneous	42	5	11	58
Total	175	244	277	696

Source: European Economic Community Commission
internal document, published in U.S. Congress, Senate,
Committee on the Judiciary, Hearings, before the Subcommittee on Antitrust and Monopoly of the Committee on the
Judiciary, Senate, on S. Res. 233, 90th Cong., 2d sess.,
1969, part 7A, p. 3, 984.

TABLE 5

Transnational Collaboration Ventures in EEC According to Economic Sectors and Countries Originating Ventures, 1968

Sector	Germany	France	Italy	Netherlands	Belgium/ Luxembourg	Total
Banks & insurance	3	7	6	3	2	21
Food processing	13	5	2	10	4	34
Chemical	36	31	5	30	6	108
Electrical & electronics	25	17	12	9	5	68
Mechanical engineering & automobile	38	21	12	30	8	109
Metallurgy	21	7	4	13	2	47
Paper	6	0	2	0	5	13
Construction & construction materials	6	8	3	16	0	33
Textiles & shoes	15	16	10	4	5	50
Natural gas & petroleum	4	0	2	3	3	12
Services	19	8	3	12	1	43
Miscellaneous	0	14	7	4	2	27
Total	186	134	68	134	43	565

Adapted from A. P. Weber, "Concentrations en Europe," Direction, No. 160 (April, 1969), pp. 392-97, Tables 3-4.

but also in metallurgy and the service industries. France and
the Netherlands evince the next highest number of border-
crossing initiatives, with the former country generally following the over-all sector distribution pattern, while the latter
shows special strength in the construction and construction-
materials field. (It is interesting to note that, while British
transnational initiatives in the Common Market in 1968 covered
the whole field of economic sectors, those of the United States
concentrated on the chemical, electronics and electrical, and
mechanical-engineering and automobile industries. [7]) Italy's
unusually small number of initiatives in the chemical field
may be attributed to the strong position in this industrial
sector of the state-controlled Ente Nazionale Idrocarburi (ENI)
and Instituto per la Ricostruzione Industriale (IRI) organizations, which in 1968 also took control of Montecatini-Edison,
an extensive chemical complex that had previously been mainly
in private hands. (For details on the Montecatini-Edison case,
see pp. 86-87, below).

DISTRIBUTION BY TYPE OF COLLABORATION

        Statistical information regarding the distribution of trans-
national ventures by type, though fragmentary, does exist.
Data are available for intra-EEC wholly and jointly owned
subsidiaries, as well as for financial participations during the
1959-66 period. As Table 4 indicates, of the 696 transnational
ventures recorded during these years, 277 are jointly owned
subsidiaries (39.8 per cent), 244 are wholly owned subsidiaries
(35.1 per cent), and 175 are financial participations (25.1 per
cent). The 1968 CEPES study adds collaboration agreements
without financial participations and "failures" to the break-
down, but excludes wholly owned subsidiaries. Its data stem
from 1,136 existing, but not necessarily new, cases in which
the main activity was centered within the Common Market
but some of the partners were also located outside the EEC.
The number of failures reported is apt to be too low, however,
since failures are rarely widely publicized. [8]
        The figures, as presented in Table 6, show that 44.2 per
cent of the border-crossing ventures were collaborations
without financial participations, 11.9 per cent included such
participations, 42.4 per cent were jointly owned subsidiaries,
and 1.5 per cent were failures. Although the above figures
are merely suggestive and cannot be correlated satisfactorily,

TABLE 6

Transnational Collaboration Ventures in EEC
According to Type

Country of Main Activity	Collaboration Without Financial Participations	Collaboration With Financial Participations	Jointly Owned Subsidiaries	Failures	Total
Germany	150	40	135	12	337
France	152	40	125	1	318
Italy	106	9	59	2	176
Netherlands	48	20	88	1	157
Belgium/ Luxembourg	46	26	75	1	148
Total	502	135	482	17	1,136

Source: Comité Européen pour le Progrès Économique et Social [CEPES], Grenzueberschreitende Unternehmungskooperation in der EWG (Stuttgart: Forkel Verlag, 1968),
pp. 208-13.

they indicate that inclusion of wholly owned subsidiaries in the
CEPES study statistics would result in a substantial reduction
of the percentages of the other categories. [9]

MAJOR MOTIVATIONS FOR COLLABORATION

As noted earlier, the prospect of a unified market, offering fresh opportunities for increased sales and permitting
cost reductions by making use of the economies of scale and
more efficient allocation of resources, is an important factor
in the rising trend of transnational business collaboration in
the Common Market. That this has been indeed a major
motivation for border-crossing collaboration agreements is
confirmed by interviews with executives of firms engaged in
transnational ventures and by the CEPES survey. [10] The EEC
treaty itself has been a reinforcing factor, for it provided a
measure of assurance for a definite direction in economic development and thereby constituted a risk-reducing element
in the calculations of firms considering collaboration ventures.
Underlying the aspirations for increased sales and reduced costs has been the powerful inducement of maximizing
profits; but, it would be an error to assume that maximizing
profits is the sole or even predominant factor in decisions to
engage in transnational collaboration. A survey of ninety-two
American and eighteen foreign multinational companies made
by Arthur Stonehill and Leonard Nathanson regarding the
criteria used for direct foreign investments discloses that
objectives in the area of production, inventory, sales, and
market share also play very significant roles in such investment decisions. [11] The authors suggest that, instead of the
traditional objective of profit maximization, "the goal of
market share subject to various economic, political, and
social constraints seems to typify the behavior of many
multinational companies" when making these decisions.
These findings seem to apply also to many decision-
making situations concerning transnational collaboration ventures, even if they do not involve any investments. Of course,
cost reductions through economies of scale and other means
remain a potent motivation for border-crossing ventures and,
in fact, may contribute to both the attainment of an enlarged
market share and the maximization of profits, although increased size does not always correlate with increased
profits. [12]

Another motivation for transnational business collaboration is the desire to combat what is perceived occasionally as
the "economic colonization of Europe by foreign capital. "[13]
Clearly, it is the large and continuing American investment
in the Common Market in the form of subsidiaries or acquisition of existing companies that is the main source of apprehension for many European executives. Over the years, American-
owned or -controlled firms have been able to capture an
increasing share of the market within the EEC. But it is not
so much the total volume of business captured by these firms
that worries the Europeans, but, rather, that U.S. investment
is concentrated in the so-called growth industries. More than
half of its investment is in the petroleum, chemical, automobile, and machinery industries, with the electronics,
precision-engineering, and food-processing industries also
being preferred targets. These industries require extensive
research and development expenditures, are capital intensive,
and are based on mass production and mass consumption.

An additional concern for European business executives
is the increased profit that American firms in Europe are able
to generate compared with that of their European competitors.[14]
For all these reasons, transnational joint ventures by European firms capable of benefiting from the economies of scale
seem to many European businessmen to be the answer for
meeting the American challenge and the way not only to retain
existing market shares, but also perhaps to recapture what has
been lost to American firms.

It is not quite clear, however, whether the economies of
scale that may be gained through collaboration ventures are
actually needed in all cases in the EEC to create optimal production conditions. The vast majority of businessmen and a
number of economists seem to clamor for greater size of
enterprises, if not, in fact, giant concentrations. But some
economists do not see such a necessity--at least not across
the board--and contend that this is a mystique motivated
mainly by businessmen's fears of increased competition after
the national tariff barriers have been removed inside the
Common Market. H. W. de Jong, a Dutch economist, argues
that for many industries optimal production conditions are
found in the medium-sized, if not small, plants and that even
such mass-production industries as steel and automobiles do
not require large-scale plants to obtain optimal conditions.[15]

In this connection, it is important to note that demand for
goods in the Common Market is not uniform, because the
culture of the EEC countries is not homogeneous. As a

consequence, the tastes and habits of consumers differ along
national and traditional lines. This factor may also reduce
the opportunities for full application of the economies of scale
for optimal production conditions. If de Jong and like-minded
economists are correct, however, border-crossing collaboration ventures between medium-sized or small companies may
achieve optimal production conditions with relative ease in
certain industries and may compete successfully with much
larger national and transnational enterprises.

A final motivation for transnational business collaboration
is essentially ideological; namely, to assure the continuous
progress of integration and thereby the future of Europe. [16]
There is a clear understanding among top-level executives of
companies engaged in transnational ventures that the interlacement effect created by the various transnational activities
is a significant factor in the regional integration process.
Most of them are personally interested in strengthening the
solidarity of the economies of the EEC member states and in
promoting a community spirit and climate. A statement made
many years ago by Professor Paul Reuter of the Law Faculty
of the University of Paris that "it is the industrial leaders
who will build Europe"[17] may well prove to contain a measure
of truth in the years to come.

RANGE OF OBJECTIVES

The particular objectives of the collaboration ventures
vary. The closest kind of collaboration involves the joint
rationalization and specialization of production, either by
assigning the manufacture of whole products or the production
of parts of a particular item to the various plants of the
partners. Another method is the establishment of a jointly
owned subsidiary to which the manufacture of either one or
several products is assigned. The advantages of the latter
method are the sharp delimitation of tasks and responsibilities
among the partners, a clear delineation of the risks of the
partners, a relatively easy accounting of costs and profits,
and a fairly uncomplicated evaluation of the success of the
collaboration. The establishment of a jointly owned production
subsidiary in an EEC country other than that where the main
plants of the partners are located adds to the interlacement
effect of the collaboration.

The over-all advantages of collaboration and division of
labor in the field of manufacturing are not only opportunities

for optimum production runs (depending on the minimal optimum plant size for a particular industry) but also shared
development costs and risks, as well as shared know-how.
(The local partner can also contribute his special knowledge
about the labor market, labor conditions, and local financing
possibilities.) As a result of the specialization that the partners undertake in the manufacture of their products, it is also
possible to introduce a higher degree of automation into the
manufacturing process, which is often essential for the effective mass production of certain goods and which, in turn, per-
mits more competitive pricing. In the event that the collaboration partners have established a joint production subsidiary,
collaboration may also lead to diversification of products and
perhaps markets. Wholly owned subsidiaries also provide
some of the advantages described above, especially the possibility of larger production runs for certain items. (It should
be recalled that wholly owned subsidiaries were classified as
transnational collaborations. [See p. 5, above.]) In addition,
they may take advantage of differences in national wages,
skills, and transportation costs--advantages that would, of
course, also accrue to other forms of transnational activities.

     Although production collaboration ventures undoubtedly
engender the highest interlacement effect, the most frequent
objective sought is the establishment of joint marketing
arrangements permitting the partner located in one country
to use the sales and service facilities of the partner in the
other country, as well as the possible employment of joint
facilities in the remaining EEC countries. Thus, the potential
for EEC market penetration by the collaboration partners is
enhanced and may, in turn, assist them in attaining market
positions in the entire EEC similar to those they hold in
their own national markets.

     But the motivation for transnational marketing arrange-
ments may also be defensive. The management of a company
may be afraid that competitors may get a head start in the
newly unified market of the EEC and thereby threaten their
national market positions.[18] Since the opening and penetration
of markets in neighboring EEC countries often require considerable investments in new marketing organizations in these
countries, as well as considerable expenditures for advertising,
transnational collaboration may be a means to avoid at least
part of these costs. Moreover, the counsel of the local partner may be useful in reducing the risks of psychologically
unsuitable sales and advertising methods. Of course, for
some companies cost considerations may be less important

than full control of marketing organizations in other EEC
countries. For this reason, they may prefer the establishment of a wholly owned subsidiary, in which case its manager
very frequently a citizen of the host country, provides the
necessary advice regarding local conditions and habits. In
some cases, collaboration partners and wholly owned subsidiaries may operate side by side, as in the border-crossing
venture between Fiat and Citroën, which will be discussed in
detail later. (See pp. 37-38.)

Transnational marketing collaboration among several
manufacturers is often combined with production collaboration,
as described earlier, or becomes the first step for such a
collaboration. Each partner limits himself to the production
of those items for which he has the most technical know-how
or that he can produce at the lowest cost. The collaborating
firms market, then, not only their own products, but also
those of their partners, enabling them to offer an integrated
range of well-balanced, highly competitive items in the EEC
countries. Depending on the specific legal provisions in the
countries of the partners, this arrangement may make it
possible to enter very competitive bids for purchases by
their governments that stipulate preferences for domestic
suppliers. Finally, this kind of collaboration may offer advantages for sales to Communist countries if the government
of one of the partners maintains especially good relations
with one or more Communist countries or has a particularly
favorable commercial agreement with it. [19]

A last category of transnational marketing arrangements
is collaboration between a manufacturer in one EEC country
and usually exclusive sales agencies (often wholesale distri-
butors) in other Common Market countries. These arrangements, called vertical collaboration, offer manufacturers
necessary information about market conditions, advertising
methods, and credit problems, while they enable the sales
agency to become well acquainted with the technical intricacies
of the manufacturer's products. Some manufacturers in the
EEC seek to create a network of bilateral vertical collaboration arrangements with sales organizations in the Common
Market and are prepared to deepen the collaboration through
financial participations, establishment of jointly owned re-
tailing enterprises, and participation of dealers in trade-mark
ownership and protection.

Another frequent objective of border-crossing collaboration is the creation of joint research and development operations. Research and development play an essential role for

the maintenance and improvement of the competitive positions
of many companies in a highly innovation-oriented and
technology-based economy. But the cost of research is high,
especially in such sectors as aerospace, electronics, and the
chemical industry, and joint ventures, therefore, may bring
research within the reach of an expanded circle of Common
Market companies. Moreover, the cost of basic research is
so astronomical that only large enterprises can usefully join
in collaboration activities in this area. Collaborative efforts
in applied research, however, may be feasible and beneficial
for many smaller companies as well; such efforts, in time,
tend to spill over to other functional areas of the firms involved, leading eventually to collaboration in production and
marketing.

The desire to close the technological gap between Europe
and the United States and to meet the powerful competition
by non-EEC and especially American companies, reinforced
by the ideological motivation of "building Europe," provides
considerable impetus for the conclusion of research collaboration agreements.[20] Barring these and other measures, the
existing gap between Common Market and American enterprises in certain industries--for example, electronics--is
bound to widen rather than to narrow. Some segments of this
industry, such as data-processing, are becoming a near
monopoly of American firms and European companies controlled
by Americans. For this reason, the EEC Commission has
recently urged Common Market firms to agree on joint research and development in the electronics field, which, hopefully, may also be backed by short-range national research
and development programs in the member states.[21]

Research and development collaborative efforts frequently
emerge from transnational agreements to exchange or acquire
licenses. These agreements, whose initial interlacement
effect is minor, usually involve interchanges of experience
with the utilization of the licenses and thereby often lead to
closer collaboration endeavors.

Two additional objectives of transnational business collaboration deserve to be mentioned. One quite important
objective is the improvement of the credit position of one or
the other partner in order to finance plant expansions or long-
term delivery contracts. Sometimes one partner may guarantee bank loans of the other. Of much less significance is the
second objective, the creation of collaborative purchasing
arrangements, unless such arrangements constitute a complementary element for production or perhaps for research
and development collaborations.

The objectives discussed should not be considered as representing an exhaustive list. Other possibilities may emerg Moreover, any combination of objectives is conceivable when two or more companies negotiate a border-crossing collaboration agreement. According to the CEPES study, which surveyed 1,448 cases of collaboration, the distribution of objectives was as follows: marketing, 469; joint production, including license agreements, 342 (263 cases were mere license agreements); research and development, 297; and purchasing, 28. Some of the arrangements had multiple objectives, and in 588 cases the sources did not specify the objectives of the collaboration.[22]

CHOICE OF LEGAL FORMS

Collaboration ventures can be cast in a variety of legal forms. The greatest flexibility is found in arrangements that leave the corporate structures of the partners untouched. This enables the participating firms to collaborate on specific functions, perhaps for a limited time, and then to dissolve these agreements without major damage to the participants. Marketing, advertising, and purchasing may be some of the specific functions undertaken on this basis. Under such an arrangement, the partners also avoid tax burdens, which usually accompany the dissolution of existing corporations and the establishment of new ones, as would be the case in mergers or the creation of holding companies and subsidiaries. Loose arrangements may also serve as a proving ground to test the compatibility of two firms and their objectives when considering a subsequent merger. No uniform corporation law exists yet in the Common Market that subjects the conclusion of mergers to great difficulties, a topic that will be discussed later.

In the event that financial participation is part of a collaboration agreement, the principle of strict division of top management among the collaborating entities, characteristic of such a venture, may be somewhat impaired in practice. This is not only the case when collaborations involve medium-sized and smaller firms, but also when transnational ventures among large enterprises include financial ties. In fact, the size of the companies engaged in collaboration does not appear to be a relevant factor when it comes to determining the choice of the collaboration form. MAN and Saviem, foremost German

and French truck manufacturers, have chosen a loose collaboration form without financial participation; Farbwerke
Hoechst and Roussel-Uclaf, very large German and French
enterprises in the chemical and pharmaceutical fields, have
a collaboration agreement with financial investment by Hoechst
in the French firm; Fiat and Citroën have formed a holding
company; and Agfa and Gevaerts have established two separate
corporations.[23] All these collaborations will be examined
later in detail. (See pp. 34-40, below.) Other aspects of
the size of the collaborations are also treated below. (See
pp. 47-48.)

Loose forms of transnational collaboration ventures also
lend themselves to linking government-owned enterprises
with private firms. An example is the collaboration between
MAN and Saviem, 84 per cent of which is owned by Renault, a
government-owned enterprise. This kind of collaboration
can operate between two government-owned firms as well.
A case in point is the transnational venture between the Italian
firm Alfa-Romeo, part of the state-controlled IRI, and Renault.
Although neither of these collaborations involve financial participations, investment ties can become part of the transnational ventures between government-owned and private enterprises.[24]

A special advantage of transnational collaboration, especially in one of its looser forms, is the adaptation of an
enterprise to the new environment created by the Common
Market. For this purpose, a company may be active in
several collaboration ventures, either in different countries
or even in the same EEC country. For example, a large firm
such as Farbwerke Hoechst has several kinds of such ventures in France, each in a different legal form and with different partners. This points up the crucial task of finding the
right partner. Poor judgment in the selection of a partner
may be one reason for the eventual failure of the collaboration.

SELECTION OF PROPER PARTNER

In order to ensure a careful selection of a partner for a
transnational collaboration agreement and also to promote
more border-crossing ventures, a number of organizations
have dedicated themselves to act as collaboration brokers.
Perhaps the most advanced organization of this kind is the
Rationalisierungs-Kuratorium der Deutschen Writschaft (RKW),

located in Frankfurt, Germany. RKW, supported by public
funds and operating for the public interest, has been active
since 1965. It cooperates closely with interested public agencies in the Netherlands, France, and some non-EEC European
countries, but its objectives are not limited exclusively to
transnational collaboration. In fact, so far, more intra-
German collaborations have been achieved than have transnational ventures, but this is understandable in view of the
difficult nature of negotiating border-crossing agreements,
especially among smaller firms. Medium-sized and smaller
companies are the main "clientele" that RKW seeks to serve,
since these firms do not possess the informational managerial
resources to evaluate fully the compatibility of a prospective
partner.

RKW publishes a quarterly list of firms interested in
finding a transnational partner and often adds foreign firms
to its national list, which appears much more frequently.
No charges are made for the listing, nor are any costs involved if a firm wants to avail itself of the counseling services
existing in all states of the German Federal Republic. More
than fifty chambers of industry and commerce and several
industrial interest groups have joined the efforts of RKW.
Collaboration partners are sought for all objectives described
above except financial arrangements, which are of a particularly sensitive and confidential nature.

Other organizations that have undertaken tasks similar to
those of RKW are the powerful Dresdner Bank in Germany and
the Diet of German Industry and Commerce. The Diet also
cooperates with local chambers of industry and commerce,
providing for their efforts a national and international information outlet. Finally, the French-German Committee for
Economic and Industrial Cooperation, which has its main seat
in Paris and which is closely tied to the two main German and
French industrial associations--Bundesverband der Deutschen
Industrie (BDI) and Confédération Nationale du Patronat
Français--has also become active in promoting individual
collaboration ventures between German and French firms.

A 1969 survey among French firms showed that more
than 100 were actively looking for a German partner. These
companies ranged in size from some with an annual sales
volume in excess of $20 million, a larger number with sales
in the $1-$20 million bracket, and the comparatively small
remainder with less than $1 million sales. The range of
industries represented among the French firms was relatively
wide. In the lead were metal-processing and engineering firms

Textiles and automotive manufacturers were close runners-up, but there were also producers of toys, furniture, food stuffs, and pharmaceuticals, as well as enterprises in the leather, construction, plastics, and electronics industries. According to the survey, these companies were seeking mainly, at the initial stage, commercial and financial arrangements, often to be supplemented by an exchange of technical information. But many looked on such collaboration as only the beginning that might lead eventually to a closer understanding, especially if an appropriate corporate form could be found.[25]

In order to meet the needs of Common Market companies seeking transnational collaboration, it has been suggested that, instead of the essentially national or binational organizations described above, a European Industrial Marriage Bureau would be more useful. Such a bureau would have several tasks. Its first task would be to build up a bank of information on European businesses, so that it could quickly provide industrial enterprises who apply for this information with a systematic picture of the potential partners in their own sectors. It is especially the medium-sized and smaller companies seeking partners that lack an appropriate network of contacts and therefore badly need this information.

The second major function of this bureau would be to act as an honest broker between companies seeking collaborating partners in other countries. As such, the bureau could explore independently the minds of potential partners in order to discover which are interested in transnational collaboration and which have genuine complementary capabilities. Moreover, the bureau could propose solutions to problems that deadlock negotiations and that companies are sometimes unwilling to discuss frankly with their partners. Many smaller companies lack the expertise of negotiation that the bureau could provide.

Its third task would be to provide expert managerial consulting service on the legal, fiscal, and managerial problems of transnational mergers. It would not be the task of the bureau to carry out all the detailed tasks of drafting intercompany agreements, but it would play a crucial role in advising on the strategic decisions suitable or needed for each type of transnational collaboration.

The fourth contribution of the bureau would be to provide financial assistance to overcome the short- and medium-term need for capital if financial participation is desired. The bureau could be endowed with a sum of capital from which it would be authorized to make loans, guarantee loans, and perhaps even make investments in enterprises with which it was concerned.

The legal status of the bureau will be crucial in establishing a good working relationship with both private industry and government. One suggestion, designed to ensure the bureau the support of industry, is that it should be a purely private venture established with private capital. But this idea has two main shortcomings. First, any private-venture institution would almost certainly tend to be linked to certain particular groups of banking and industrial interests. It would not be trusted by, or available to, all. Second, a private venture would not be able to reflect and stand for the broader European public interest that needs to be considered and emphasized.

Two possible alternatives would be to make the bureau a wholly public institution or to make it a combined public-private body, with the first alternative as perhaps the most suitable and appropriate. In that case, the bureau would be set up under a convention or protocol to the existing European Community treaties and would be run by an executive director appointed by the Council of Ministers upon proposals of the EEC Commission. The role of the bureau may well be crucial for the industrial European Community policy advocated by the Commission, which will be discussed in detail in Chapter 3.[26] (See pp. 99-101.)

TECHNIQUES OF COLLABORATION

Border-crossing collaboration between entities in different countries, by its very nature, requires a high degree of coordination. In turn, a high degree of coordination can be achieved only if the channels of communication between the staffs of collaborating enterprises function smoothly and effectively. It is difficult enough to find optimal solutions for these organizational goals within the national framework. If one adds differences in languages, traditions, and habits of the staff members concerned with the collaboration, it becomes obvious that coordination and the proper communications are complex tasks whose achievement may be costly and for which patience and a certain amount of experience are needed. Although a pragmatic approach to coordination is advisable, questions regarding this aspect of collaboration, as well as the problem of communications, must be carefully examined and settled in detail at the time the collaboration

agreement is negotiated. This is especially important when
the collaboration objectives are joint marketing and production
ventures.

The larger the companies engaged in the collaboration
venture, the more levels of coordination need to be organized.
On the top management level, periodic meetings must be set
up between the collaborating firms to evaluate the success of
the venture and to eliminate, as early as possible, any misunderstandings, which have a way of creeping into transnational undertakings. In large companies a high-ranking exexu-
tive, close to the chief executive, is usually appointed as
main liaison officer, and he is assisted by a staff official who
is charged with the coordination of the collaboration activities.
The coordination itself is carried out through various committees and working groups composed of officials of the
collaborating firms. The specific functions of the committees
and working groups depend on the nature, scope, and level
of the collaboration. The committees normally engage in
operations and staff work and may be charged with the determination of production goals and methods, marketing problems,
and other activities. In the working groups technical details
are worked out in which engineers often play the major role.
In collaborations involving smaller companies, the owners
and managers are the chief liaison and coordinating officials.
In all transnational ventures it is essential that the officials
performing on the same level also have equivalent ranks and
that the impression is never created of one partner's not
fully respecting the other or seeking to dominate him.

The coordination and communications problem is less
acute when collaboration is to be carried out within the framework of a jointly owned subsidiary. In such a subsidiary,
officials of both partners are normally active in both management and operations. This fact alone is likely to ensure a
steady flow of information to the principals about the status
and development of the collaborative ventures. Similarly,
financial participations tend to strengthen the coordination
and communications machinery of a collaboration, because
the need for strict financial accounting introduces additional
links between the partners, particularly if the accounting
habits differ in the countries involved and if fiscal laws are
at variance. Moreover, financial participation by one or the
other partner is likely to deepen the collaborative effort and
may thereby reduce the chances of communication and coordination breakdowns.

CASE STUDIES

MAN/Saviem

To furnish a greater insight into the techniques used in transnational collaboration, it may be instructive to examine briefly a few actual cases. As previously noted, the agreement between MAN of Germany and Saviem of France is an example of collaboration without financial participation. (MAN is controlled by Gutehoffnungshuette, a German holding company with interest in machinery, engineering, and metal products. It is the fiftieth largest industrial group outside the United States. Saviem is owned by Renault, which is the nineteenth largest company outside the United States.[27]) The agreement, concluded on February 21, 1968, has as its major objectives to strengthen the competitive position of the partners and to share with their customers the benefits flowing from the rationalization of production and research. (The agreement, which took nearly five years to negotiate, runs until December 31, 1982. Unless notice for termination is given by December 31, 1979, it continues in force but can be canceled after three years' notice.)

For the attainment of these objectives, collaboration between the two companies extends to research and development, division of labor in the manufacture of parts and certain types of trucks, and sales and services for all trucks produced jointly or individually. MAN assembles the trucks whose parts are produced jointly for the German market, and Saviem is charged with assembly of these trucks for the French market. (The trucks whose parts are produced jointly range from 7.5 tons to 19 tons. Smaller trucks are manufactured exclusively by Saviem, larger ones by MAN.[28]) Even before the conclusion of the collaboration agreement, however, MAN and Renault, Saviem's parent company, were linked by a license agreement. Moreover, since spring, 1967, MAN has represented Saviem in Germany as sales agent for trucks up to 7.5 tons.

The marketing arrangements of the collaboration agreement provide that the sales and service organizations of the two companies in Germany and France offer an integrated line of trucks manufactured by them, as well as services for their products. As a consequence, 750 service centers are available in both countries. In addition, some elements of a collaboration venture between Renault and Alfa-Romeo, dating

back to 1959, are tied in with the MAN/Saviem arrangement.
(Alfa-Romeo ranks 185 among the 200 largest companies outside the United States. The agreement with Renault had some
joint production features, but it was mainly focused on the
rationalization of marketing. Today, however, Renault and
Alfa-Romeo have separate distribution networks for their
passenger cars in France and Italy.) Alfa-Romeo produces
certain motors for Saviem with MAN-patented carburation
systems, but the use of the Alfa-Romeo distribution net for
the sale of Saviem and MAN trucks is much more important.
(Saviem also has its own distribution subsidiary in Italy,
Saviem-Italiana.)

As far as exports to other countries are concerned, the
marketing organization of either one or the other company is
used, depending on which has proven itself most effective in
a particular state. This method is especially beneficial for
MAN in African countries, formerly French colonies, but may
also prove advantageous for the partners in Eastern Europe,
where in some countries French products are more welcome
than are German goods. The good connections of Alfa-Romeo
with Communist countries are also useful for MAN and Saviem
trucks.

Each company has appointed a staff coordinator who reports to, and works very closely with, one or more top-level
executives. Various coordinating committees, composed of
members of both companies, have been established in different
functional areas, such as production and advertising. Engineering and administrative working groups operate under
these committees. About 120 people from both partners are
involved in the coordinating scheme.

The chief coordinators and key personnel of the committees meet once a month, either in Paris or in Munich. Attor-
neys are usually part of the delegation, since the contract
between the two companies requires continuous adaptation to
changing production and marketing conditions. A bond of
personal friendship has grown up between the two chief coordinators and their families, and this bond is a significant
element when it comes to solving problems that crop up between the partners.

Farbwerke Hoechst/Roussel-Uclaf

The joint venture between Farbwerke Hoechst of West
Germany (one of the world's largest chemical concerns, ranking number sixteen among non-U.S. firms) and Roussel-Uclaf

(France's second largest pharmaceutical company) is an example of a collaboration agreement with a financial participation. Hoechst acquired an indirect interest of about 20 per cent in the French company through the purchase of about 40 per cent of Compagnie Financière Chimio of Paris, a privately owned holding company that controls Roussel-Uclaf.

The agreement, concluded for a ten-year period and renewable for similar periods, covers joint research, production, and marketing efforts throughout the world. All new products developed by either firm, as well as revenue derived from licensing fees, will be shared between the two companies. Hoechst has been given two seats on the twelve-man board of directors of Roussel-Uclaf and the president of the French firm has been elected to the board of Hoechst.[29] Clearly, financial participation by its nature requires closer ties. The negotiations aimed initially at the conclusion of a license agreement, but their scope was expanded when it was discovered that there was a high degree of complementarity in the products of the two companies.

The channels of communications established by the cross appointments of high-ranking officials of both companies to their respective boards constitute an important instrument for top-echelon coordination. For operational coordination, Hoechst and Roussel-Uclaf have created four main committees dealing with research and development, sales, production, and economic policy. Below this level are a number of working groups concentrating on details. About fifty or sixty persons are involved in coordinating activities. Meetings of the committees alternate between Paris and Frankfurt, and top executives also make frequent visits to the headquarters of their opposite numbers.

The collaboration with Roussel-Uclaf is not Hoechst's only transnational activity in France. Another collaboration agreement with the French firm Nobel-Bozel was announced in March, 1969. In addition, four wholly owned marketing subsidiaries were set up earlier, and three jointly owned production subsidiaries operate in which Hoechst owns shares ranging from 25 per cent to 50 per cent. To coordinate the various transnational ventures in France, Hoechst uses a special, wholly owned subsidiary.[30] Other transnational collaboration ventures of Hoechst in the Common Market are located in the Netherlands, where the German company has a wholly owned and a jointly owned subsidiary.

Roussel-Uclaf also has a second collaboration venture with a German firm, C. F. Boehringer, an important

manufacturer of pharmaceutical products. The objectives of
this venture are joint production and the sale of the German
products through Roussel-Uclaf marketing channels in a number of countries. Hoechst supports this collaboration in the
field of research. The three companies form the largest
European chemical and pharmaceutical group and are capable
of offering strong competition to the American giants in these
sectors.

Fiat/Citroën

Undoubtedly the greatest public interest aroused by a
collaboration agreement of two Common Market firms was
that between Fiat and Citroën in autumn 1968. Two factors
accounted for the widespread attention that this event received almost daily in the press for a number of weeks. The
first was the extent of the venture. Fiat is the largest producer of automobiles in number of units in Europe--second
in terms of dollar sales volume after Volkswagen--and Citroën
is number seven. Fiat already controls truck and tractor
manufacturing plants (Unic and Someca) in France. Citroën
possesses a 99 per cent stock control of Berliet, foremost
producer of heavy trucks; in turn, 62 per cent of Citroën is
owned by Michelin, the prominent French tire manufacturer.[31]
(Of the 200 largest industrial enterprises outside the United
States, Fiat ranks number thirteen; Citroën number thirty-
five; and Michelin, number fifty-nine. Volkswagen is, at
present, number five, but the combination of Fiat and Citroën
exceeds the sales of Volkswagen and would, in fact, put it in
third place in terms of dollar volume after the Royal Dutch/
Shell group and Unilever.[32] It will also be the third largest
producer of automobiles in the world, behind General Motors
and Ford, but ahead of Chrysler. The second factor was the
initial opposition of the de Gaulle Government to the collaboration agreement, because it appeared to threaten the independence of a very important French industrial company. The
political aspects of this venture will be examined in detail
later. (See pp. 62-63)
The Fiat/Citroën agreement is an example of transnational
collaboration involving a complex financial participation scheme
and the creation of a holding company to implement this
scheme. The holding company controls about 62 per cent of
Citroën stock, and Fiat, in turn, owns 24 per cent of the
holding company, with the remainder of the shares held by the

Michelin and Berliet families, as well as possibly others. [33]
The new combine has also taken control of Maserati, Italy's
luxury-car manufacturer, through acquisition by Citroën of
50 per cent of Maserati's capital, as well as of Ferrari,
Italy's foremost sports-car producer. [34] Rumors exist that
Fiat has or is about to buy the Lancia auto works, third
largest producer of automobiles in Italy.

The holding-company arrangement is designed to enable
Fiat to play a significant role in the affairs of Citroën without
impairing the formal independence of the latter. This aspect
was essential in order to counter the political sensitivity of
the French Government regarding the collaboration arrangement. For this reason, the agreement specifically does not
apply to Citroën's military manufacturing subsidiary, Panhard-
Levassor. Management decisions for this company remain
the exclusive competence of the Panhard executives and the
French military authorities.

The collaboration objectives of the two companies are in
the fields of research, production, investment, purchasing,
and marketing. The full program of joint activities is expected to be implemented over a period of six years. The
first collaborative efforts were made in the areas of research
and purchasing. Since spring, 1969, Citroën dealers in
France and Belgium have begun to distribute a first model of
Italian manufacture, which is produced by the Fiat subsidiary
of Autobianchi. It is not yet clear, however, whether, in
due time, the sales organizations of both companies will offer
all models manufactured by them or whether distribution of
various models will be carried out on a selective basis. The
rationalization of production between the two partners appears
to be two to three years away.

To coordinate the far-reaching transnational activities
planned, a comprehensive committee and working-group system
is envisaged, but its full institutionalization has not been completed. In the meantime, joint planning is carried out on the
top management level, while coordination in fields where
collaborative efforts have begun is effected on lower staff and
technical levels. The establishment of a jointly owned special
unit for the purpose of managing and supervising the coordination effort is also under consideration.

Agfa-Gevaerts

Apart from full acquisition, perhaps the closest kind of
transnational collaboration and the best-known case of a

border-crossing venture in the Common Market is the affiliation between the German firm Agfa A. G. and the Belgian
company Photo-Produits Gevaerts S. A., dating back to July,
1964. The two firms, the most prominent producers of
photographic equipment in Europe (the combine ranks number
162 in the list of the 200 largest corporations outside the
United States), established in each country a new corporation
the Agfa-Gevaerts A. G. in Germany and the Gevaerts-Agfa
N. V. in Belgium, each of which has the same capitalization
and is equally owned by the founding companies.

Both of the new companies have the same management and
substantially the same board of directors and both have taken
over all activities of the old companies. (German law requires representation of labor on the board of directors, but
this is not the case in Belgium. Agfa stock is controlled by
the powerful chemical group of Bayer, but no influence is
exercised on the manufacture of the Agfa-Gevaerts combine.
The importance of this factor will be discussed later. [See
pp. 45-48.]) Since the consummation of their marriage,
Agfa-Gevaerts have engaged in additional transnational ventures with three French firms through acquisition of majority
stock control. These ventures have enabled Agfa-Gevaerts
to enlarge their line of copying equipment for business use and
have enhanced their potential for obtaining a larger share of
the market.

It is evident from the close affiliation between the two
partners that the collaboration objectives cover all fields.
The results have been generally beneficial. Production runs
of some items could be stepped up in different German and
Belgian plants, whereas others were discontinued. The fusion
of the two world-wide distribution networks also yielded significant advantages.

Despite the close affiliation of the two companies, close
coordination of the activities of the two partners was found to
be essential. The techniques for coordination follow the
usual patterns of an extensive two-level committee system
composed of officials from both companies. The four top-level
committees are chaired by high-ranking executives, who may
even be members of the board of management. These committees deal with such matters as production, sales, advertising, and other functions of a strategic nature. The lower-
level committees are chaired by middle-rank officials, and
there is an overlap of committee membership to ensure optimum communications between the coordinating committees.
Also for this reason, the chief coordinators of both firms serve

on several committees. The meetings of the committees are
usually held halfway between the headquarters of the two
companies in a motel, which bears the suggestive name of
"Euromotel. "

The pattern of techniques used for transnational business
collaboration revealed in the four cases related above has
been confirmed in the interviews with executives of other companies engaged in border-crossing ventures. The utilization
of these techniques can also be discerned when one examines
the thirty cases of transnational collaboration surveyed by
the CEPES study. [35] Clearly, in order to ensure proper control and attainment of the collaboration objectives, coordination and excellent communications between the partners must
have a very high priority, regardless of the form used for
the venture. Otherwise, the chances for failures increase,
because a variety of typical problems, many of which arise
from a lack of circumspection and foresight on the part of
management, are apt to beset the transnational activities of
the partners.

COLLABORATION PROBLEMS

The problems of transnational collaboration stem from
the very nature of the joint enterprise. They can be broken
down into four broad categories: socio-psychological factors,
conceptual differences with respect to business methods,
divergences in the goals and expectations of the partners, and
politico-psychological grounds.

Socio-Psychological Factors

As pointed out earlier, the culture prevailing in the EEC
countries is not homogeneous. Although the countries have
common historical roots, the evolution of the nation-state in
Western Europe has produced strongly particularistic traditions and habits that continue to persist even though their
force has been weakened by the existence of the Common
Market, Eurotelevision, and an unprecedented and continuing
travel wave throughout Europe. In particular, the existence
of four different languages in the Common Market remains a
significant barrier to smooth social interaction, and problems
arising from the differences in languages have plagued transnational business collaboration.

In some cases the language problem has been especially bothersome on the highest management level, where both precision of expression and considerations of prestige play a very important role.[36] Although many high-echelon executives have a working knowledge of the partner's language, the right nuances may be necessary to convey the exact meaning of a legally or administratively significant statement. To ensure this effect fully, an individual may have as his only recourse to resort to his mother language. One could argue that the use of interpreters could surmount this difficulty, but this is often frowned upon, since it could jeopardize the secrecy of the discussions. It is for these reasons that Farbwerke Hoechst has insisted on a crash language-instruction program in Paris for one of their top executives involved in the collaboration with Roussel-Uclaf. And it is for the same reason that the president of the French company, Jean-Claude Roussel, takes a daily one-hour lesson in German.[37]

The language barrier has been less of a problem on the middle management level, which is concerned with the day-to-day operations and staff tasks of the collaboration. In many cases, younger individuals are involved on that level; they are often chosen for these tasks because of their linguistic capabilities or their willingness to learn the language of the other partner. In the joint committee meetings of the Agfa-Gevaerts collaboration it is not unusual that the Germans and the Belgians use their own languages, which are sufficiently understood by their counterparts. (This multilingual procedure is now frequently used in conferences of European academicians.)

The differences in languages, however, are not the only problems in the socio-psychological area. World War II is not yet forgotten, especially by those who participated in the fighting--either actively as soldiers or passively as civilian targets of bombs and other military actions--normally the older generation, whose members still occupy many leadership positions in Common Market enterprises. Their attitudes remain fixed by long-standing prejudices, although for a number of top-ranking executives the war is a positive motivation to engage in collaborations, in order to build a unified Europe and not to be faced again with intra-European struggles. Many top-level officials of Roussel-Uclaf at first opposed collaboration with a German firm, preferring American, British, or Italian firms. They have since become convinced, however, of the advantages of the joint venture with Hoechst.

But prejudices are not only related to the war. The different development of national cultures has led to a variety of stereotype images of the nationals in different EEC countries that are not conducive to fruitful collaboration. Thus, for example, there is the image of the industrious and disciplined German versus the Italian more oriented toward the dolce vita, and the intellectual and individualist Frenchman versus the frugal, hard-headed Dutchman. These images may be reinforced when an official of one company suffers "cultural shock" through an extended stay at the offices or plants of the transnational partner.[38] Already existing inferiority and superiority complexes are apt to be strengthened. But, extensive interaction between officials of the partners may also have a contrary effect through greater understanding of the culture of the partner's country. It may, in fact, serve as a challenge to overcome the old images and prejudices and to accept the values and group norms prevailing in the society of the partner with objectivity and equanimity.

Whatever the outcome, the socio-psychological problems should not be underestimated for the proper functioning of transnational collaboration ventures. A survey of nearly 500 Dutch enterprises engaged in transnational collaboration ventures in the Common Market, undertaken by H. W. de Jong and M. Alkema of the Europa Institute of the University of Leyden, suggests that these problems occupy a very significant place among the difficulties that some of these firms (about 25 per cent) have encountered in their ventures. The experience of these Dutch companies reveals that this type of problem showed up with the relatively highest frequency with partners in France, somewhat less with those in Belgium and Italy, and least with German collaborators.[39] Although, according to this survey, these difficulties have induced only a few companies to terminate border-crossing ventures, their existence has been a major motivation for refraining from entering into a transnational collaboration agreement that was under consideration.[40] Clearly, the incidence of socio-psychological problems is closely related to the intensity of nationalism prevailing in a particular country. Although nationalistic tendencies continue to persist in all Common Market countries, the emergence of France as the country in which Dutch firms have encountered most of the socio-psychological difficulties is not surprising.

Conceptual Differences Regarding Business Methods

Cultural differences and national traditions are also underlying reasons for problems and misunderstandings caused by
disparities in the notions of how to conduct business, both
from an operational as well as an administrative view. Dis-
similarities in the educational programs of the EEC member
states and variances in the training requirements for executive positions also contribute significantly to these difficulties.
Moreover, accounting habits and calculations of costs and
profits often vary from country to country.

Perhaps the greatest problems arise from the differing
willingness to use communications channels fully and frankly
and from divergent views regarding conference and negotiation
tactics. Whatever the objectives of the collaboration, complete information pertinent to the attainment of these objectives must be made available by the partners. Conferences
and negotiations may fail if one partner, following long-
standing practices and traditions, seeks to approach the core
of the subject by various detours and flourishes of rhetoric
while the other wants to come to the point immediately. Moreover, words and actions may convey different meanings to the
partners, and the effects that follow may be quite at variance
with expectations.

Finally, the relationships between top-echelon executives,
those who exercise highest control and have ultimate responsibility, and lower-echelon managers and staffs vary at times
between the EEC countries. For example, in Germany and,
without doubt, in Italy the distinction between the two echelons
is more rigorous than it is in France; as a consequence the
leadership style in the first two countries may be more in-
dividualistic than it is in French enterprises.[41] There are
indications that smaller enterprises, particularly those that
are family-owned and "one-man" operations, suffer more
from these problems than do larger firms, which can avail
themselves of professional management. Again, older men
in managerial and staff positions seem to have been troubled
to a larger extent, because to them the questions of national
habits and traditions appear to be more weighty.

Although the particularistic cultures, traditions, and
habits prevailing in the EEC countries undoubtedly ill prepare
business executives for transnational collaboration, it is
important to stress that with careful coordination and the use
of effective communications channels many conceptual problems have ultimately been overcome. Especially where

positions in the committee system have been held by younger
men, the collaborative activities have moved along quite
smoothly, despite differing mentalities and professional
jealousies, which seem to have been more pronounced among
engineers in technical working groups than among other
functional committees.

Conceptual differences have been side-stepped by tolerance and understanding of the cultural background and tempera-
ment of collaborators of other nationalities. A desire to be
flexible and to engage in true give-and-take has often produced
genuine comradery among the members of a committee or a
working group. It has created the feeling among them of belonging to a multinational, if not "European, " group with
shared goals and has opened up communications going beyond
those usual among co-workers.

The continuous interaction necessitated by the transnational collaboration ventures have provided opportunities not
only to understand better the traits peculiar to other nationals
in the Common Market countries, but also to appreciate the
values attached to these traits. In some cases highly personal
ties have been established among members of the coordinating
groups, and visits between families of committee members in
their respective houses are not uncommon. For example, the
chief coordinators of Saviem and MAN always dine in the house
of their counterparts during the monthly visits. In addition,
the Saviem coordinator, who did not speak German and had to
depend on the French-language capability of his MAN counterpart to conduct the almost daily telephone conferences and
monthly face-to-face negotiations, insisted that his son learn
German and that the young man spend his summer vacations
as an apprentice in the MAN plant in Munich.

If one considers that up to 200 individuals may be active
in each coordinating system of a transnational collaboration
venture, one may assume that a subtle political socialization
process is operating, through which a very gradual adoption
of "European" values and beliefs may take place. Of course,
the experiences flowing from coordinating activities are not
intended to have political effects, nor are these effects immediately recognized. Nevertheless, they have latent
political consequences, because the individuals involved in
this process may relate these experiences to their political
environment. To a great extent, committee and working-
group members participating in the coordination activities
of a border-crossing collaboration may "socialize themselves. "[42] (Individuals socializing themselves adopt, thereby,
new values and beliefs of a political nature.)

A positive though subtle influence toward the adoption of "European" values and norms may also be exerted by leaders of companies engaged in joint ventures who are outspoken in their support for European integration. Such leaders may take on the role of "socializing agents." One example is Giovanni Agnelli, the chairman of the board of Fiat, who not only has expressed himself with great vigor on many occasions for moving European unification forward, but also has explicitly stated that the collaboration with Citroën was motivated strongly by this goal.[43] Another example is Karl Winnacker, president of Hoechst, who is equally interested in the pursuit of this goal and who is surrounded by a remarkably Europe-oriented top leadership group.[44]

Divergences in Goals and Expectations

Another problem area, also related to some degree to the cultural differences found among the managers and staff of firms collaborating across national borders, stems from divergences in goals and expectations of the partners. These divergences may pertain to the distribution of profits, the competition of the collaborating enterprises in certain markets, the organization of research, the competence of the coordination mechanism, or the application of technological know-how to different production facilities of the partners. In some cases, one partner may have been motivated to enter the collaboration agreement by essentially defensive considerations, such as to eliminate the other partner as a competitor on the home market. If the latter, however, is bent upon pursuing a very aggressive marketing strategy and sales do not rise sufficiently to satisfy his earlier expectations, the collaboration will be in trouble. In other cases, one partner may want to benefit from the economies of scale in production by being able to offer the jointly produced goods at lower prices, whereas the other partner may be interested in, and expect, mainly higher profits or enlarged markets.[45]

In this connection, an example of the MAN/Saviem collaboration is noteworthy. One of Saviem's goals was to sell its line of smaller trucks through the MAN marketing organization in Germany. Some of the district sales offices of the German firm, however, are beginning to refuse to promote the sales of these French vehicles energetically, because they are considered unsuitable for certain German markets. The MAN district sales managers have recommended certain

modifications in the Saviem line of trucks, but, so far at
least, the French company has declined to act on these recommendations, preferring to remedy the situation by sending
special teams of troubleshooters to visit various MAN district
sales offices.

Conflicts of interest and disappointed expectations are apt
to create mistrust and disillusion, which, in turn, can be
dangerous for the success of a collaboration. Of course,
changing conditions may modify goals and expectations, and
then the scope of a collaboration venture may need to be
altered or reduced. This was the case in the joint venture
between Alfa-Romeo and Renault, which began as a marketing
and limited-production arrangement in the passenger-car
field and now is focused only on certain collaborative efforts
in the truck category.

Goals and expectations may also be at variance when two
companies have established a joint subsidiary in the country
of one of the partners. In such cases it is sometimes difficult
to draw clear lines between the production and marketing
policies of the subsidiary and of the partner operating in the
same country as the joint venture. Unless it is possible to
delineate clearly the goals and interests of both partners and
to safeguard the latter, the confidence between the partners
may erode rapidly.

It is evident, then, that, if border-crossing collaboration
ventures are to be successful, common interests must be
clearly defined and recognized. This highlights the need for
a most careful selection of partners for such ventures and
thorough consideration and airing of all problematic questions
prior to the conclusion of the agreement. This does not mean
that all questions have to be definitively settled; in fact, the
settlement of some questions may be left open until after some
practical experience has been gained. The issues should,
however, be fully understood and should at least have been
examined in the light of the interests and goals of the partners
concerned.

In the selection of partners, personal relationships appear
at times, to play a significant part, even when large companies
are involved. Roussel-Uclaf at first sought collaboration with
American firms, later with British and Italian companies, but
could not find the proper partner. Exploratory talks were
held with the German chemical firms BASF (Badische Anilin
& Soda Fabrik) and Bayer, but the former was considered too
nationalistic and the latter not sufficiently flexible. Hoechst,
the partner finally chosen, appeared to be internationally

minded and Europe oriented. The fact that the director of the
Hoechst sales organization in France had since school days
been a close personal friend of Jean-Claude Roussel, president of the French firm, may have exerted an important influence in this choice.

Similarly, in the MAN/Saviem collaboration, an official
of the German firm who had worked with Saviem prior to and
during World War II--and who was very favorably inclined
toward France in general--may have been an influential factor
in inducing the MAN top management to enter into negotiations
with Saviem regarding a possible collaboration venture.
Nevertheless, the negotiations dragged on for nearly five years
because differing goal conceptions had to be reconciled.
Finally, it is noteworthy that Umberto Agnelli, the brother
of Fiat's chairman of the board, Giovanni Agnelli, was president of Fiat-France (the twenty-sixth largest French corporation) prior to and during the time of the negotiations with
Citroën. It is not clear, however, what role Umberto Agnelli
played in the motivation and selection of Citroën as Fiat's
partner.

Experience has shown that the prospects of success for a
transnational collaboration venture are enhanced when the
collaborating firms are about the same size and that they are
reduced in cases where relatively small firms are involved.
This is especially true in "one-man" or family operations,
where the main interest is to provide a good income and
representative positions for the members of the family. The
question of size is important in this instance because on this
factor may well depend the attainment of maximum benefits
from rationalization measures.

Another consideration of size involves the apprehension
by firms of being placed in the position of the "weaker" partner, which might lead to a take-over by the stronger collabora-
tor. The problem of size has, so far, prevented the Dutch
automobile manufacturer DAF (Van Doorne's Automobilfab-
rieken) from entering into a collaboration agreement, although
its management has been actively seeking a suitable partner.
Lancia of Italy had been considered, but, because of the
strong similarity in the passenger-car models of the two
firms, a successful collaboration was placed in doubt. In the
meantime, DAF has bought motors from Renault on an outright
purchase contract for some of its models, but, because of
the difference in size between the two companies, no full-
blown collaboration agreement was envisaged as beneficial.

In order to reach the proper size to collaborate effectively on the European scale with an appropriate firm of another nationality, some companies have first sought mergers on a national level. Whether a firm will turn to searching for a transnational partner once it has expanded its size through a successful national merger is hard to predict. The trend toward national mergers in Common Market countries was strong during the late 1960's; witness, for example, the mergers in the German automobile industry (Volkswagen-NSU [Neckarsulmer Motorenwerke]), in the Belgian steel industry (the Cockerill group and Evence-Coppé), and in the French chemical industry (Pechiney-Saint-Gobain with Ugine-Kuhlmann)[46] These actions may well be symptomatic of some very large companies in the EEC that are trying to build up their size within their national boundaries without any intention of engaging later on in border-crossing collaboration ventures.

Politico-Psychological Problems

Finally, disparate developments in the political culture of Common Market member states have a bearing on relations between companies and governmental agencies. As a consequence, the style of these relations differ from country to country, and these differences may well cause problems for transnational collaboration ventures. In France, for example, a high degree of technocratic solidarity appears to prevail in relationships between firms and the bureaucracy, which is reinforced by the high qualifications of the higher civil service and, consequently, greater dependence on officialdom. In Italy, the style of these relationships is strongly affected by the existence of powerful public holdings in industry and commerce, such as IRI and ENI.[47]

Since the establishment of jointly or wholly owned subsidiaries in any of the EEC countries requires obtaining licenses or permissions from the public authorities, contacts with the bureaucracy may have to be frequent. But, even in collaborations that do not involve the establishment of subsidiaries, the need may arise for a variety of bureaucratic contacts; at a minimum, governmental consent is necessary for certain types of foreign investments. Of course, it is in this type of collaboration that the foreign partner hopes to benefit from the good relations that the local partner may have with governmental authorities and institutions in his country.

It is significant, in this connection, to stress the differing expectations that nationals in various countries have regarding the amount of consideration that they may receive
from officials for their points of view. According to a five-
nation survey made by Gabriel Almond and Sidney Verba, 53
per cent of the respondents in Germany expected "serious"
consideration; 18 per cent, "little attention"; and 5 per cent,
"to be ignored." In Italy, the corresponding percentages were
35, 15, and 11. (The percentages for Great Britain were 59,
22, and 5; for the United States, 48, 31, and 6; and for Mexico,
the fifth nation surveyed, 14, 48, and 27.[48]) In the previously
discussed survey by de Jong and Alkema of Dutch enterprises
engaged in border-crossing ventures, France was mentioned
by six respondents and Italy by two as countries where politico-
psychological difficulties were encountered.[49]

As noted earlier, the subtle process of political socialization may contribute gradually to surmounting some of the
problems flowing from differences in national culture and
traditions, as well as their effects on the entrepreneurial
climate and business-related behavior in the Common Market
countries. Another resource in this direction may be the
European Institute of Business Administration (INSEAD) in
Fontainebleau, which is modeled after the Harvard Graduate
School of Business Administration and emphasizes the European dimension in its instruction. (INSEAD also publishes
a monthly management review called European Business.)
Its graduates may eventually fill important staff positions
in companies operating on a European scale and may assist
in overcoming the conceptual differences and national tendencies regarding business methods that have been troubling some
of the transnational collaboration ventures.

Recently, a number of national business administration
schools have agreed to stress a uniform European orientation
in instructional programs, which would increase the flow of
junior business executives into positions where a commitment
to "European" values and beliefs may be highly significant.
It is fair to assume that many of these executives, as they
reach top-level positions, will carry with them the "European"
spirit and, in the event that they are employed in firms concerned with transnational activities, they are likely to contribute as "socializing agents" to the acceleration of the
political socialization process operative there.

VIABILITY OF TRANSNATIONAL COLLABORATION

The problems discussed in the preceding pages have raised doubts in the minds of some business executives about the viability of collaboration ventures that leave the corporate structures of the partners untouched and operate with a divided top management. It is argued that these problems weaken the coordination that is sorely needed under such management conditions and that, as a consequence, the effective rationalization of production and marketing methods suffers. For example, attempts to assign the production of specific items to the plant of a partner capable of producing these items at the lowest cost and the highest quality may be resisted because the partner in question is accustomed to manufacturing traditional items for its traditional markets, or the item to be produced may be less profitable than the traditional products.[50]

Although it cannot be denied that, under certain circumstances, unified management through merger of two entities or other means may indeed be preferable, it is precisely the flexibility of the loose collaboration venture that induces a company with various important assets in its own country to seek the benefit of partnership with a firm in another EEC country without having to give up its identity.

The task of the managements of the partners, therefore, must be to elaborate a clear definition of their common interests and objectives prior to the conclusion of the collaboration agreement and to manage the coordination activities so efficiently that the necessary control and success of the rationalization measures envisioned in the agreement will be ensured to the highest degree. This task may, at times, tax the imagination and try the patience of the management, but the interviews done for this work and the case studies performed by the CEPES survey suggest that, in most instances, the obstacles to coordination can be overcome with tolerance, good will, and long-term persistence.

Despite the collaboration problems discussed so far and the essentially political impediments that will be examined in Chapter 3, the upward trend of transnational collaboration continued in 1969. Some of the firms participating in this trend were very large: for example, Union Chimique Belge (UCB); the Dutch chemical group Algemene Kunstzijde Unie N. V. (AKU); and the German Glanzstoff A. G., engaged in transnational collaboration that resulted in the emergence of a new giant in the chemical industry, with approximately 80,000 employees and sales exceeding \$2 billion. The legal form used followed the example set by Agfa-Gevaerts. (See pp. 38-40.)

Another important collaboration agreement utilizing the same legal form was concluded between Fokker Aircraft of the Netherlands and Vereinigte Flugtechnische Werke of Bremen, Germany. Although the principals of this collaboration were Dutch and German, Belgian and French interests were also involved, inasmuch as Fokker controls 50 per cent of a Belgian aeronautical company, the S. A. Belge de Constructions Aeronautiques, while the other 50 per cent is owned by the French company Marcel Dassault. Finally, the Dutch steelmaker Hoogovens and the German steel firm of Hoechst engaged in a joint venture during 1969. Both companies are prominent enterprises in the Netherlands and Germany and have a combined total of 77,000 employees. A number of additional collaboration agreements between important Dutch and German firms that were concluded in the first six months of 1969 suggest a growing interlacement between the enterprises of the two countries and a continuation of a trend beginning in 1968, as indicated in Table 3, above. [51]

It should be noted, however, that national collaborations and mergers also continue to make a very strong showing, often with the blessing and active stimulation of some of the EEC member governments. An outstanding example is the take-over of NSU by Volkswagen in the first part of 1969. This was effected by the merger of NSU with Auto-Union, a wholly owned Volkswagen subsidiary. About 140,000 employees were involved in this merger, which gave Volkswagen control of about 56 per cent of West German automobile production. It prevented Fiat from obtaining the licenses to the rotary-piston Wankel engine that NSU holds.

Another large company that pursued an active national merger and acquisition policy has been Rhône-Poulenc in France. [52] This firm has acquired certain chemical interests of three other French companies--Pechiney, Saint-Gobain, and Ugine-Kuhlmann. The result has been a major industrial reorganization in France, bringing greater coherence to the relatively fragmented state of the French chemical industry and increasing its competitiveness vis-à-vis the German and American chemical giants.

NOTES

1.   See, for example, Fortune's biannual listing since
1963 of the top 200 industrial companies outside the United
States.

2.   These figures stem from a survey of collaborations
listed in 1968 and 1969 in the Annex on Economic Interpretatio
of the Agence Europe Bulletin.   These figures may not include
all collaborations, but nevertheless they seem to be suggestive.   See also "Trois mariages par jour," Communauté
Européenne, No. 140 (March, 1970), p. 19.

3.   See U. S. Department of Commerce, Survey of
Current Business, XLIX, 9 (September, 1969), 20.

4.   European Economic Community Commission internal
document, published in U. S. Congress, Senate, Committee
on the Judiciary, Hearings on Economic Concentration, before
the Subcommittee on Antitrust and Monopoly of the Committee
on the Judiciary, Senate, on S. Res. 233, 90th Cong., 2d
sess., 1969, part 7A, p. 3,984 (hereafter cited as Hearings).

5.   For a similar survey for 1967 using somewhat different criteria, see A. P. Weber, "Les mouvements de concentration en Europe et la pénétration industrielle et commerciale," Direction, No. 148 (March, 1968), pp. 262 ff.

6.   Comité Européen pour le Progrès Économique et
Social (CEPES), Grenzueberschreitende Unternehmungskooper
ation in der EWG (Stuttgart: Forkel Verlag, 1968), p. 206
(hereafter cited as CEPES study).   The cases were culled
from European newspapers and professional journals dating
back over several years.   The information received from
these sources was supplemented by a number of interviews
with business executives.   In 1,136 cases the main activity
is within the Common Market, but transnational relations
exist also with enterprises in non-EEC countries; 706 cases
are concerned exclusively with intra-Common Market ventures.   Thirty case studies are published in detail.

7.   A. P. Weber, "Concentrations en Europe," Directior
No. 160 (April, 1969), pp. 392-97, Tables 3-4.

8. See CEPES study, pp. 51-54.

9. See also Weber, "Concentrations en Europe," pp. 396-97.

10. See CEPES study, p. 17.

11. Arthur Stonehill and Leonard Nathanson, "Capital Budgeting and the Multinational Corporation," California Management Review, X, 4 (Summer, 1968), 39-54.

12. See Hearings, part 4.

13. André Marchal, "Necessité Économique des fusions et concentrations intracommunautaires," Revue du Marché Commun, No. 109 (January-February, 1968), p. 31.

14. See CEPES study, pp. 149-57; and Rainer Hellmann, Amerika auf dem Europamarkt (Baden-Baden: Nomos Verlagsgesellschaft, 1966), especially pp. 214-27.

15. See the testimony of Professor H. W. de Jong in Hearings, part 7, pp. 3608-36. See also the testimony of Jacques Houssiaux, in ibid., pp. 3583-3608, and his "Limites économiques des concentrations et fusions," Revue de Marché Commun, No. 109 (January-February, 1968), pp. 51-82; and Harald Jurgensen and Hartmut Berg, Konzentration und Wettbewerb im Gemeinsamen Markt-Das Beispiel der Automobilindustrie (Goettingen: Vandenhoeck and Ruprecht, 1968).

16. Marchal, op. cit., pp. 44-48.

17. Quoted in ibid., p. 44.

18. See Sanford Rose, "The Rewarding Strategies of Multinationalism," Fortune (September 15, 1968), pp. 100 ff., especially pp. 101-2.

19. See CEPES study, pp. 30, 39, and 79-82.

20. See Marchal, op. cit., pp. 45-48.

21. Journal of Commerce (September 26, 1969).

22. CEPES study, p. 206.

23.   See CEPES study, p. 25.

24.   For example, see Johannes Meynen, Wolfgang Friedmann, and Kenneth Weg, "Joint Ventures Revisited," Columbi Journal of World Business, I, 2 (Spring, 1966), 21-22.

25.   Journal of Commerce (December 1, 1969).

26.   See Christopher Layton, European Advanced Technology--A Programme for Integration (London: George Allen and Unwin, 1969). See also Christopher Layton, "Trois idées pour une stratégie industrielle," Communauté Européenne, No. 139 (February, 1970), p. 6; and his discussion paper for the Conference on European Industrial Integration, February 23, 1970.

27.   Fortune (August 15, 1969).

28.   For additional details, see the special edition of the Handelsblatt on German-French commerce (June, 1968), p. 15

29.   International Herald-Tribune (October 2, 1968).

30.   Le Monde (October 22, 1968) and Agence Europe Bulletin (March 28, 1969).

31.   Le Monde (October 30, 1968).

32.   See Fortune (August 15, 1969)

33.   International Herald-Tribune (October 29, 1968) and Le Monde (October 30, 1968).

34.   International Herald-Tribune (March 13, 1969) and Journal of Commerce (October 22, 1969).

35.   CEPES study, pp. 77-144.

36.   In this connection, see the pertinent comments by Michel Drancourt and Henri Lepage, "Obstacles psychologiques (et politiques) aux concentrations et aux fusions intra-communautaires," Revue du Marché Commun, No. 109 (January-February, 1968), pp. 137-39.

37.   See Le Monde (October 22, 1968). When the author interviewed Mr. Roussel in May, 1969, a large blackboard with German phrases in his office was clear evidence that the lessons were continuing.

38.   See Pierre Tabatoni, "Remarques sur les obstacles psycho-sociologiques à la cooperation internationale," Revue du Marché Commun, No. 109 (January-February, 1968), pp. 99-104.

39.   H. W. de Jong and M. Alkema, Revue du Marché Commun, No. 109 (January-February, 1968), p. 152.

40.   Ibid.

41.   See Tabatoni, op. cit., p. 100.

42.   See Richard E. Dawson and Kenneth Prewitt, Political Socialization (Boston: Little, Brown and Co., 1969), pp. 38-39; and Gabriel A. Almond and Sidney Verba, Civic Culture (Boston: Little, Brown and Co., 1965), pp. 266-306.

43.   International Herald-Tribune (January 17, 1969).

44.   Express (France) (December 9-15, 1968).

45.   See CEPES study, pp. 68-73.

46.   See International Herald-Tribune (March 8, 1969); Agence Europe Bulletin (March 10, 1969); and Francis M. Goldmark, "Europe Catches the Merger Fever," Columbia Journal of World Business, IV, 2 (March-April, 1969), 49-54. See also H. Peter Dreyer, "EEC Key to European Mergers," Journal of Commerce (March 8, 1966).

47.   See Tabatoni, op. cit., pp. 100-101.

48.   Almond and Verba, op. cit., p. 72.

49.   De Jong and Alkema, op. cit., p. 157.

50.   See Meynen, Friedmann, and Weg, op. cit., pp. 24-26.

51.   See also Le Monde (March 16-17, 1969); Agence
Europe Bulletin (March 24, 1969); International Herald-
Tribune (May 13, 1969); Sueddeutsche Zeitung (July 17, 1969);
and Communauté Européenne, No. 129 (April, 1969), p. 27,
No. 130 (May, 1969), p. 21, and No. 131 (June, 1969), p. 19.

52.   International Herald-Tribune (March 8, 1969 and
June 10, 1969); and "L'Europe des entreprises en Marché, "
Communauté Européenne, No. 136 (November, 1969), p. 30.
For explanations of this phenomenon, see H. W. de Jong,
"Specialisation, concentrations et Marché Commun, " Revue
de l'Économie du Centre-Est, X, 40 (April-June, 1968),
pp. 195-213, especially p. 197.

CHAPTER **3** POLITICAL ELEMENTS:
NEW PRESSURES AND
OLD REALITIES

Although the roots of not only the politico-psychological
difficulties but also the other problems examined in the last
chapter stem largely from factors outside the operations of
border-crossing ventures, i.e., cultural differences and
divergences in national habits in the EEC member states, it
is the interaction between executives and staff members of
the partners within these ventures that produces the problems.
This chapter will begin with an examination of difficulties and
impediments to successful collaboration that are essentially
different, inasmuch as they are caused in their entirety by
factors outside the collaboration operations. These are mainly
obstacles growing out of actions and nonactions on the part of
the national authorities in the member countries and, to a
lesser degree, the European Community institutions, especially the Council of Ministers and the EEC Commission.

Impediments to the free flow of capital and goods affect
collaboration plans and their implementation perhaps most
immediately. These obstacles can be broken down into several
categories. First, transnational investments continue to be
subject to some administrative control by the member governments, although the scope of this control varies from one member to another. Second, despite the elimination of the tariff
barriers in the intra-Common Market movement of goods,
differing fiscal laws and technical standards, as well as varying
administrative regulations and practices, create delays at the
borders and increase the cost of goods. A third category of
difficulties stems from disparaties in the national corporation,
antitrust, and fiscal laws, which result in differing national
treatment of identical activities of the partners in several EEC
countries and impose restraints on the goals of the collaboration ventures, such as eventual mergers. Divergent labor laws
and social legislation may also fall in this category.[1] The
fourth category of difficulties, though perhaps of less direct
importance for transnational ventures, flows from differences

57

in the national economic and monetary policies of the member
states, which produce continuing uncertainties for marketing
programs and joint production schemes of the transnational
partners.[2]

To overcome these difficulties obviously requires specific
action on the part of the national authorities in the EEC member
states and/or certain Common Market institutions. As a consequence, firms interested or engaged in transnational ventures have articulated pertinent demands to obtain favorable
responses by these authorities. Although these demands are
economically motivated, inasmuch as they aim at ensuring
optimum conditions for transnational business collaboration
ventures, they seek for this purpose an "authoritative allocation of values" and thereby become political objectives. (See
p. 8, above.)

DECISION-MAKING IN EEC

The decision-making machinery in the EEC is highly complex. Although some of the Common Market institutions, such
as the Council of Ministers and the EEC Commission, are
assigned a central role in the decision-making process by the
EEC treaty, the national authorities of the member countries,
which constitute subsystems of the whole European Community
system, also play a highly influential, if not decisive, part.
The multilevel interaction and interpenetration among European
Community institutions, national governments and administrations, political parties, and interest groups in this process
are much more intensive and extensive than those usually prevailing between traditional international organizations and
national authorities or professional groups. The domestic
politics of each member state and the interstate politics within
the Common Market have a substantial bearing on the making
of specific decisions and policies in the European Community.

The complexities of decision-making have been compounded
by a shift in the balance between the Council of Ministers and
the EEC Commission that had been so carefully drawn by the
framers of the EEC treaty. This shift has resulted in a significant reduction of the effective powers of the EEC Commission
which the treaty had envisaged as the initiator of decisions and
policies, whereas the role of the Council of Ministers was
mainly to accept or to reject the EEC Commission's proposals.
The well-known resurgence of nationalism in all of the member

states, rekindled principally but not exclusively by the phil-
osophies and actions of President De Gaulle, bears a major
share of responsibility for this development.

As a consequence, the Committee of Permanent Representatives, composed of national civil servants and subordinated
to the Council of Ministers, has assumed an increasingly larger
part in the decision-making process of the European Community. Conversely, the EEC Commission has been limited during
the latter half of the 1960's mainly to technical operations, the
collection of information, and the preparation of reports, with
its political influence cut substantially. Of course, it continues
to possess the functions assigned to it by the treaty, but, as
the result of the political conditions prevailing since 1965, the
EEC Commission has exercised these functions with restraint
and a measure of passivity. Since de Gaulle's resignation from
the presidency of France, however, the EEC Commission has
begun again to display a higher degree of activism. As far as
other major Common Market organs that participate in the
decision-making process are concerned, i.e., the European
Parliament and the Economic and Social Committee, their
legal powers are very restricted and their effective powers
are even weaker. [3]

In view of the complex decision-making process in the
European Community, firms interested or engaged in border-
crossing ventures can either address their demands directly
or channel them indirectly through interest groups and political
parties to the national administrations, as well as to the EEC
institutions. If addressed directly or channeled to the national
administrations, interest groups, parties, and national bureaucracies perform the function of "gatekeepers," to use David
Easton's terminology. As such, they control the flow of pertinent demands, which, as a consequence, may be enhanced,
killed, delayed, or modified. Similar functions may also be
carried out by European-level interest-group federations such
as UNICE (Union des Industries de la Communauté Européenne),
the subdivisions of the EEC Commission, the Committee of
Permanent Representatives and its working groups, and others. [4]

The Council of Ministers has the final decision-making
authority, but, when this body issues directives to the EEC
member governments, their execution depends on the bureaucracies of the national administration. These groups are thus
able to exercise their gatekeeping power a second time. (When
the Council of Ministers promulgates a "regulation," however,
it is "binding in every respect and directly applicable in each
member state," according to Article 189 of the EEC treaty.)

This power includes decisional latitude as to the form and
means for the implementation of the directive; the authority
to interpret its meaning, through which both the thrust and the
details of the implementation can be influenced; and simply
procrastination in carrying out the directive.

The particular demands actuated by transnational business
collaboration and the specific objectives pursued vary, depending on whether they are to be obtained prior to or after
the conclusion of the collaboration agreements. The examination of these objectives and their attainment potentials will
begin with the precollaboration period.

PRECOLLABORATION PERIOD

In order to conclude collaboration agreements, some kind
of authorization of the national governments in whose territorie
the firms involved are located may be required when financial
participations of one prospective partner in the enterprise of
the other are to be made. As noted earlier, all member goverï
ments exercise some administrative control over foreign investments. In Belgium, Germany, and Luxembourg the criteri
of control seem to be more general, whereas in France, Italy,
and the Netherlands they are more specific in distinguishing
between the more welcome and the less desirable foreign investments. But, even in those countries where authorization
is mainly a formality or is only required for special cases,
the national governments tend to oppose informally substantial
investments that are regarded as adverse to the "national
interest."[5]

The requirement of authorization seems to contravene the
aim of the EEC treaty, which, in Articles 67-73, insists on
the progressive abolishment of restrictions on capital movements within the Common Market except in the event of temporary balance-of-payment and other difficulties. Specifically,
these clauses seek the elimination of any discriminatory treatment of persons or firms based on nationality, place of re-
sidence, or the place in which capital funds are to be invested.
(The EEC Commission has recently charged that a French law
of January, 1969, requiring prior authorization by the French
Ministry of Finance for all investments in France by foreign
companies, including those from EEC countries, violates the
EEC treaty. It has taken action to bring this violation before
the European Community Court.)[6]

Most of the member governments are apprehensive however, about large outflows of capital, since they may hurt their
social and economic policies. Moreover, they prefer these
funds to be invested in their own countries to assure maximum
employment.[7] The concern of the governments is especially
pronounced when investments in prominent national firms by
companies of other EEC countries might signify a shift of
control. The persistance of the national perspective, the burden of the protectionist past, and the uncertainty about the
future of Europe reinforce the attitudes of the member governments, which have a decided predilection for national solutions
for collaborations among enterprises.[8]

It is noteworthy that the German Government introduced
early in 1970 a bill to control all new mergers that would require prior authorization for companies interested in such
cooperation. Although this bill is aimed mainly at strengthening
the antitrust provisions in West German law and has application
only for German territory, it may well unfavorably affect initiatives for transnational collaboration.[9] (Certain exceptions
to this control are included in this bill, especially with respect
to mergers necessary to maintain competitive positions against
foreign firms.) In this connection, a study dealing with mergers
and cooperations made by the Ministries of Economic Affairs
and Justice in the Netherlands emphasizes the problem of
maintaining the national character of some large Dutch groups
and the social problems that may be caused by a reduction of
the labor force in the event of business cooperation. Although
no specific recommendations were made to solve these problems, the tenor of the study could be significant.[10]

The foregoing should not be taken to mean that consent
for financial participations in border-crossing ventures is
generally refused; in fact, in the majority of cases permission
is eventually granted. For example, in the late 1960's French
authorities only rejected between four and six requests annually
from foreign firms for financial participations in French companies.[11] Nevertheless, these rejections suggest some reluctance on the part of member governments for this type of
activity and their desire to supervise and regulate it. For this
reason, in all cases requiring government authorization, its
procurement has highest priority, and political influence and
pressure must at times be exerted to achieve this objective,
for without it the collaboration venture cannot be started.

Pressures and Counterpressures: Fiat/Citroën

One of the best illustrations of the problems encountered in obtaining government consent can be found in the conclusion of the collaboration agreement between Fiat and Citroën in October, 1968. The intricate nature of that agreement has already been described. (See pp. 36-38, above.)

In Italy the leftist unions and political parties opposed the collaboration agreement on the grounds that the massive out-flow of capital resulting from it would harm future Italian employment and economic development prospects, especially in the South. Nevertheless, the Italian Government gave its full approval to the agreement, with only a little persuasion on the part of Fiat.

To obtain the French Government's consent was a much more difficult undertaking. The final decision was that of President de Gaulle, whose government announced on October 10 that it objected to the financial arrangements of the agreement, which could unfavorably affect the independence of an important French industrial company.[12] Renault and Peugeot, France's other two major automobile producers, may have had a hand in the rejection, because they feared stiffer competition as the result of the Fiat/Citroën collaboration. These two companies, which already engage in some cooperative pursuits together, proposed a three-way arrangement with Citroën in which they would have a major voice. But Citroën rejected this alternative. Some of the French unions, especially the powerful, Communist-oriented General Confederation of Labor, also strongly opposed the Fiat/Citroën agreement and expressed fear of grave repercussions on the employment of French labor.

Condemnations of the French Government's decision were voiced all over Western Europe, including France. The Italian Government, in particular, deplored the French decision and considered it another veto in Common Market affairs.[14] The EEC Commission raised the question whether the French decision were not placing into doubt the principles of free movement of capital as stipulated by the EEC treaty.

In France the powerful Confédération Nationale du Patronat Français added its support to the agreement through the issuance of a statement by its president denouncing the interference of the government in collaboration projects among private firms. And Valery Giscard d'Estaing, prominent French political leader and Finance Minister of the first post-de Gaulle Government, declared that the "Common Market makes no sense if governments bar across-the-border mergers."[15]

On October 25, the French Government reversed its initial decision, after the prospective partners had revised their agree· ment by reducing Fiat's planned financial participation in the joint enterprise. This reduction of Fiat's financial interest apparently dispelled the French Government's fears of a threat to the ownership or control of France's second largest auto manufacturer. In response to the apprehension expressed by French labor unions that Citroën would cut its work force or that an Italian-controlled company would give priority to the employment of Italian labor, a communiqué issued by Citroën and Fiat pointed out that the collaboration of the two firms should permit an increase of their competitive position, which was the sole guarantee of the stability of employment and future growth.[16] The widely voiced criticism and various pressures exerted in France itself however, most probably played an equally important role in persuading the French Government to tolerate a Fiat presence in Citroën. The original French veto had been interpreted in many quarters as a major obstacle to the construction of Common Market-wide companies, capable of meeting international, particularly American, competition.

With the necessary authorization granted, the Fiat/Citroën agreement was seen as a major step toward Common Market industrial integration across the national boundaries of the EEC countries. And success often begets success. A few weeks after the conclusion of the Fiat/Citroën agreement, Pirelli, the big Italian tire manufacturer associated with Fiat, and Dunlop (France), whose main headquarters are in England, announced a collaboration agreement aimed at the production and sales of certain Dunlop tires by Pirelli and the production and sales of certain Pirelli tires by Dunlop.[17]

Case of Failure: CFP-GBAG

The attempt by the Compagnie Française des Pétroles (CFP) to obtain a 30 per cent participation in the Gelsenkirchener Bergwerks-AG (GBAG) is an example of unsuccessful political pressures exerted for the procurement of government approval for a transnational business collaboration venture. This was to be done through the acquisition of a large bloc of shares held by the Dresdner Bank of West Germany that the bank was willing to sell. The GBAG is principally a coal-mining concern; however, it also owns petroleum resources in Lybia, possesses substantial refinery installations, and participates in the control of a widespread marketing organization for gasoline and oil products.

The French Government supported the CFP in its endeavor and hoped for approval by the West German Government, particularly after it had consented to the collaboration venture between Farbwerke Hoechst and Roussel-Uclaf, which had involved a significant financial participation of Hoechst in the French firm. Although President de Gaulle and the Minister of Economics and Finance, François Ortoli, lobbied strongly during their semiannual meeting with German Government leaders in September, 1968, for French-German collaboration in the petroleum business, as proposed by the CFP, and despite continued high-level pressures on the part of the French, the West German Government refused to approve it.

The professed reason for the refusal was the necessity to bring order first into the fragmented petroleum market in the German Federal Republic by pooling the interests of the German oil companies. The GBAG, as the only German oil-producing company with drilling rights abroad, was to become the nucleus for a viable German petroleum industry. After a national solution for this strategically important industry had been achieved, collaboration with EEC partners could be considered. (Interestingly, after the French veto of the Fiat/Citroë agreement, the German Ministry of Economics stressed the similarity of motivations for the French and German disapproval of the two collaboration proposals. The change of the French position did not engender a similar change in the German attitude toward the CFP proposal, however.)

Despite these understandable reasons, this is an instance where nationalistic considerations of a member government have won out. In the meantime, in pursuit of the West German Government's plans, a German consortium has purchased the bloc of shares held by the Dresdner Bank. Perhaps in order to placate the hurt feelings of the French, however, the German Government has given a French company its first contract for oil deliveries to the new German petroleum organization and has also held out hope for long-range delivery contracts to the CFP.[18]

Search for Remedies

To overcome or at least reduce substantially the obstacle of governmental authorization for financial participations in border-crossing ventures would require the full implementation of Articles 67-73 of the EEC treaty, coupled perhaps with an appropriate harmonization of economic and monetary policies

of the member governments. But, so far, very little progress
has been made in the full liberalization of capital movements
within the Common Market, and proposals by the EEC Commission dating back to 1964 have not received approval by the
Council of Ministers.[19]

One proposal for a directive setting into motion the progressive abolition of restrictions on capital movements is now
in the process of being submitted to the Council of Ministers,
and companion proposals are also being prepared.[20] Their
fate, however, is far from being certain, considering the
attitudes of most member governments. In the meantime, the
EEC Commission has engaged in additional initiatives to achieve
the creation of an integrated European capital market. This
was done in connection with the presentation of a comprehensive industrial policy early in 1970 (See pp. 98-101, below.)
and its efforts to move forward on the creation of a monetary
union. (See pp. 73-77, below.)

UNICE has expressed its full support for the efforts of
the EEC Commission to move the EEC from a customs union
to a full economic union. In a resolution published in spring,
1969, UNICE urged the member governments to pay greater
attention to the interests of the European Community and to
surmount the political obstacles impeding the functioning of
the Common Market. More specifically, the vice-chairman
of the Confédération Nationale du Patronat Français demanded
in a report to the general assembly of that organization in
summer, 1969, that the free movement of capital become a
reality and a liberal policy on foreign investments be introduced.[21]

Specialized interest groups have also urged the same objective. For example, the West German Banking Federation
has urged the early integration of capital markets in the European Community on several occasions, pointing out that such
action would stimulate integration in other sectors of the Common Market.[22] More recently, the European Center for Public
Enterprise (CEEP) adopted a position in favor of the creation
of a unified European financial market, although it suggested
some over-all control on the European level for this activity.[23]

Companies contemplating or actually engaged in transnational joint ventures, however, seem to have undertaken
only a few initiatives to seek in a general way the elimination
of approval for financial participation required by national
governments. Perhaps one example is the declaration of the
president of the powerful Société Générale de Banque, a firm
strongly engaged in transnational activities, urging the

integration of the capital markets of the six EEC member states.[24] A Similar note was struck by the annual report of another bank, the Société Générale de Belgique.[25]

But, beyond occasional declarations in support of a unified capital market in the European Community, most companies interested in transnational collaboration seem to accept national authorization for border-crossing investments as a fact of political life, although as members of the national confederations of industry, such as the Conféderation Nationale du Patronat Français or the German BDI, they undoubtedly share the sentiments expressed by UNICE and the vice-chairman of the Conféderation Nationale du Patronat Français.

CHIEF COLLABORATION OBJECTIVES

Once a transnational collaboration agreement has been successfully concluded, the main political goal of the firms engaged in border-crossing ventures becomes the creation of optimal conditions for the efficient functioning of these ventures. For this purpose, the following major objectives can be identified:

(1) complete elimination of border customs check points within the Common Market,

(2) harmonization of fiscal laws,

(3) harmonization of national laws setting technical standards for industrial products,

(4) creation of a European patent law,

(5) elaboration of a "European" company statute either through European Community regulation or through promulgation of identical national laws, and

(6) liberal àpplication of EEC anti-trust laws.[26]

These objectives are also supported by many firms not engaged in transnational ventures. They are especially significant, however, for collaborating firms because of the very direct effect that their attainment would have on the economic results of the collaboration.

Of course, the absence of common economic and monetary policies in the EEC and especially the recent devaluation of the French franc, as well as the revaluation of the German mark, are also sources of concern. They require cost and price recalculations in joint marketing arrangements and

production collaboration schemes. But the lack of assured
common economic and monetary policies does not have the
persistantly unfavorable effects on transnational ventures as
some of the other national government-related obstacles have,
nor does it reduce the options of the partners as does the absence of a uniform European company statute.

Although internal tariffs have been eliminated in the
Common Market, the customs check points continue to be
needed for several reasons. Goods imported into a member
state must be inspected for compliance with national health
and other special laws; certain taxes, such as TVA (added-
value tax) and others, have to be levied; and TVA taxes may
have to be reimbursed for goods leaving a country where such
a tax exists. The necessary delays on the frontiers are obviously costly and reduce the effectiveness of transnational
ventures.

An additional burden is imposed by the differing national
customs procedures and regulations of the member states.
Some progress was finally made, however, in spring, 1969,
in the harmonization of national customs regulations, after
many efforts dating back to 1962 had failed. The EEC Council
of Ministers adopted a number of directives to the member
governments that constitute, when translated into national
legislation, at least the beginning of a "European" customs
code. [27] Of course, this code needs to be completed and, if
past experience is any guide, this may still take a few years.

Fiscal Disparities

Fiscal harmonization has been enhanced through the introduction of similarly constructed TVA taxes in all member
states except Italy. The introduction of these taxes, however,
has tended to increase prices on the retail level and has, therefore, added to inflationary pressures already prevailing in the
EEC countries. As a consequence, the Dutch Government was
compelled to initiate temporary price controls during spring,
1969; the Belgian Government delayed the application of these
taxes until January 1, 1971, despite the serious misgivings
of the EEC Commission. [28] Italy has indicated that the modification of its tax structure and the introduction of TVA taxes
can not be accomplished until 1972, a delay strongly opposed,
but finally accepted, by the EEC Commission. [29]

The introduction of similarly constructed TVA taxes,
clearly a decisive step toward fiscal harmonization, does not

mean, however, uniform tax rates in the member countries. Therefore, if the costly delays in the movement of goods across the borders are to be eventually eliminated, these rates must be made uniform. Once this difficult process is accomplished, the member governments are under at least an implicit obligation not to change these rates by unilateral action, which constitutes an important limitation on their autonomy and sovereignty.

Moreover, since the TVA taxes are consumer taxes, a clearinghouse mechanism must be developed through which member governments can remit tax funds levied on goods shipped to another EEC state to the government of that state. The EEC Commission is now in the process of studying procedures and elaborating proposals for the progressive unification of TVA rates and the necessary mechanism to permit the elimination of border delays for the adjustment of TVA taxes.[30] Obviously, this will be a long drawn-out project whose success is anything but certain at this time.

Other impediments of a fiscal nature for transnational ventures include the differing national taxes and tax rates applicable to mergers, financial participations, and dissolutions of enterprises, as well as the double imposition of taxes on company headquarters and subsidiaries located in different EEC countries. The EEC Commission has submitted to the Council of Ministers proposals for two directives that would establish a uniform tax structure and would eliminate existing discriminations against transnational ventures. So far, no action has been taken by the Council of Ministers, since the national governments have expressed a variety of reservations.

Finally, differing national tax structures and tax rates on a variety of industrial products impose burdens on border-crossing collaboration. For example, the tax rates applied by France and Germany on the weight per axle of trucks vary greatly. This unfavorably affects the rationalization potential of the joint production and marketing arrangements between MAN and Saviem discussed earlier. The EEC Commission has, in general, supported the harmonization of the national tax systems regarding utility vehicles, and the European Parliament has taken a strong stand in favor of the EEC Commission's position.[32] At least so far, however, an appropriate directive proposed by the EEC Commission has not been adopted by the Council of Ministers.

Disparities of Technical Standards

Equally serious obstacles for transnational ventures
emerge from divergent national laws setting technical standards
for industrial products. From the MAN/Saviem collaboration
it is obvious that different French and German standards for
brakes, lights, body size, etc., can be frustrating and harmful to the full rationalization of production and marketing.
Similar problems exist not only for other industrial products,
but also for pharmaceutical manufacturers and food-processing
companies. The EEC Commission has worked up a general
program for eliminating the disparities of national laws with
respect to industrial products and processed foods that has
been accepted by the Council of Ministers and was to be implemented by the end of 1970. Numerous reservations by some
of the national delegations concerning the powers to be assigned
to the European Commission, however, and technical delays
made it clear that this deadline would not be maintained. A
new target date, the end of 1971, was set, but even this deadline may not be realistic.

The first directives implementing the program of harmonizing technical standards were issued in the automobile sector.
They dealt with such matters as levels of acceptable air pollu-
tion, permissible noise levels of engines, and common standards
for number plates and fuel tanks. It is highly significant that,
although these directives were adopted by the Council of Ministers by a unanimous vote, this unanimity had to be purchased
at the price of certain concessions concerning the European
Community procedures to be instituted and the EEC Commission's role in the event of controversy among the member
states. At the request of the French delegation, the procedures
that had been formulated earlier had to be made considerably
more flexible and appreciably reduced the European Community's
role and powers in this matter. One cannot allay the fear that
the more flexible procedures bargained out by the member
governments will form a precedent that will be followed in
similar cases of harmonizing technical standards.

Also, the directives adopted do not go into force immediately; the member governments are given eighteen months to
issue at the national level the necessary regulations for the
implementation of the European Community directives. Of
course, an additional step of coordination is required, inasmuch as the national regulations must come out at the same
time. The EEC Commission realizes this and has asked the
member governments to coordinate the dates when the common
standards are to come into force.[33]

Action, or rather nonaction, in the pharmaceutical sector has also given rise to concern about the implementation of the European Community's harmonization program. Although the Council of Ministers had already adopted in 1965 a harmonization directive in this field, it has not been implemented by some of the member countries. The EEC Commission has declared, however, that it will bring the derelict national governments before the European Community Court "if they continue to neglect their duties".[34]

Clearly, without uniform technical standards (including health regulations), there can be no elimination of border control points and, consequently, no true Common Market with full freedom of movement of trade. But serious differences of opinion continue to plague the implementation of the program adopted by the Council of Ministers. It is not easy to define the equitable point of intersection between the protection of the consumer and the demands of quality, on the one hand, and the necessity not to hinder the free circulation of goods, on the other. It often happens that some national positions put forward under the guise of consumer protection are really forms of concealed protectionism.[35]

"European" Patent

The creation of a European patent law has made progress, partially as the result of energetic demands made by Agfa-Gevaerts and supported by a number of pharmaceutical and chemical companies in the EEC. Although patents are not covered by the EEC treaty, the Council of Ministers, acting as representatives of the six member states, agreed in March, 1969, to initiate negotiations aiming at a multilateral convention through which inventors would receive patent protection in the participating countries by a single administrative act. Other European countries, notably those that have requested full or associate membership in the EEC, have been invited to join the negotiations. Later plans call for a second multilateral convention that would create a truly "European" patent.[36] It should be noted that the EEC Commission is participating in the negotiations, thereby giving them a distinct "Community" character.

"European" Company

Less promising than the developments in the patent field are the prospects for elaborating a common statute for a

"European" company. Although transnational collaboration
agreements have been successfully concluded without the
existence of such a law--in fact, most collaborations do not
aim at a merger--its absence suggests a climate of legal in-
security that is likely, in an indirect way, to act as a brake
on the trend toward border-crossing collaboration ventures
and hinders mergers where they are desired. [37]

One major source for the difficulties in evolving common
rules for a European company is the attitude of the labor unions.
In West Germany the law grants labor the right of participation
in the management of companies through the obligatory inclusion of labor representatives on the board of directors. The
German Federation of Labor and most German political parties will support a European company law only if it did not
reduce the labor participation rights presently existing in
Germany. In fact, German labor would like to have these
rights expanded. The labor unions in the other five member
states disagree with the Germans on these demands to varying
degrees. [38] The Italian labor unions actually oppose the labor
participation provisions of the German law, because they consider that sitting "on both sides of the fence" would reduce
their bargaining power.

Until the labor unions can find a compromise solution,
which also must be acceptable to the employers and the national
governments, no progress can be expected on the question of
the European company. But, even if the problem of labor
participation were solved, another hurdle--the very complex
registration system of shares in Italy, which is strongly de-
fended by the Italian Government as a means of tax control--
would have to be overcome before success could come within
sight.

Since the foregoing difficulties have made it impossible
for the EEC Commission to proceed with the elaboration of
proposals on directives covering the European company law
as a whole, it has sought to address itself to certain types of
companies and certain aspects of their activity. Pursuing
this approach, the EEC Commission has submitted to the
Council of Ministers a proposal for a directive regarding the
harmonization of legislation on companies with limited responsibility. Since the proposal is highly technical, it would serve
no purpose to discuss it within the context of this study.
Suffice it to say that it is simply a reflection of the interests
of the EEC Commission to move along on every path possible
to achieve eventually common regulations regarding a European
company law. [39]

Antitrust Provisions

In the application of the antitrust provisions of the European Community treaties the EEC Commission has a means to promote and strengthen the integrationist tendencies produced by transnational collaboration agreements. In fact, the attitude of the EEC Commission is basically liberal and sympathetic to these agreements, because it recognizes their value for the process of integration and the need for sufficiently large units that can compete effectively with the American business giants. The views of the EEC Commissioners are not uniform in this respect though, and in the opinion of several of the businessmen interviewed, the over-all tenor of the decisions handed down by the EEC Commission is ambiguous.

In an offical declaration issued in July, 1968, the EEC Commission specifically welcomed the collaboration between small-and medium-sized enterprises, inasmuch as it would contribute to an increase of their capabilities and competitive positions in an enlarged market. With respect to the collaboration of large enterprises, however, the backing of the EEC Commission was more qualified.[40] Clearly, the EEC Commission opposes all collaboration agreements that contain restrictions on the economic interchange between the member countries.[41] (In July, 1969, the EEC Commission found that several chemical companies had violated the EEC antitrust regulations and imposed relatively heavy fines. Among the fined companies were giants of the European chemical industry.[42])

An additional problem for transnational collaboration stem from the double application of European Community and national antitrust provisions, where the latter exist. For example, Germany pursues the "doctrine of two barriers," and sometimes German antitrust provisions tend to be more restrictive than the application of the European Community provisions. German firms engaged in transnational collaboration would like the European Community antitrust laws to predominate in order to avoid having to litigate on the fronts before they are assured of being in compliance with the pertinent regulations.

Coordination of Economic and Monetary Policies

Although the coordination of economic and monetary policies of the member states is not among the prime objectives of enterprises engaged in transnational collaboration,

it will be instructive for the over-all conclusions of this study
to devote some comments to the progress made in the field.
In response to coordination proposals made by the EEC Commission in February, 1969, the Council of Ministers adopted
in July of that year an obligatory consultation procedure for
the member governments. These consultations are to take
place within the Monetary Committee, the Short-Term Economic Policy Committee, and the Budget Policy Committee.
In special cases the consultations may also take place within
the Council of Ministers. The member governments are
obligated not to put national measures into force until the consultation procedure has taken place. Nevertheless, economic
policy-making remains a national prerogative and consultation
does not imply automatic harmonization. [43]

A further stimulus to the coordination of economic and
monetary policy of the member states was provided by the
summit conference of heads of state and chiefs of government
of the EEC member states held in December, 1969. One of
the main points of the communiqué published at the end of this
conference was the development of an economic union among
the EEC members, including the creation of a European Reserve Fund. Undoubtedly, the inclusion of this objective was
motivated to a great extent by the currency disturbances in
in 1968 and 1969, which were to a considerable degree the
consequence of divergent economic trends within the European
Community and which ultimately led to the devaluation of the
French franc and the revaluation of the German mark.

Recognizing that the harmonization of the disparities in
economic trends was the only alternative to a constant repetition
of these undesirable events, the Council of Ministers adopted
on January 26, 1970, an initial program of coordinating
economic and monetary policy in the European Community.
This program contained not only guidelines for short-term
economic development in 1970, but also plans for a common
definition of medium-term indicators and specific economic
guideposts for 1970-75, as well as an inventory of the main
structural reforms to be accomplished at national and European
Community levels. [44]

About two weeks later, the European Community's five
central banks (Belgium also representing Luxembourg) activated arrangements for making available $2 billion as short-
term monetary aid to member countries running into temporary
balance-of-payments difficulties. The agent for this arrangement is the Bank for International Settlements in Basel, and
drawings can be made in any currency. Although the proposed

monetary aid will not correct imbalances existing in one or more of the European Community countries, it will help a member state receiving aid to correct its imbalances without disrupting the flow of trade with the other members. In addition the availability of these short-term arrangements is an important incentive for a member country to follow the European Community's short- and medium-term economic policies, since the central banks can refuse to aid a country that has not followed these policies.[45]

In March, 1970, the EEC Commission transmitted a communication to the Council of Ministers defining the steps that would eventually lead to economic and monetary union. Three stages are envisaged: the first to finish at the end of 1971; the second, by the end of 1975; and the third, at the end of 1978. The third stage, however, could be extended by two years. The EEC Commission pointed out that balanced progress must be made between the economic union and the monetary union and that no priority should be given to one element over the other.

The EEC Commission considered as the main sectors constituting economic and monetary union: (1) the coordination of short- and medium-term economic policies, (2) the gradual creation of a unified capital market, (3) fiscal harmonization, and (4) strengthening monetary solidarity. The deadline of 1978 was chosen because it coincides with another prospective historic European Community achievement--namely, the full establishment of the European Community's financial autonomy, providing the institutions with independent financial resources to be controlled exclusively by the central European Community authorities. Moreover, this deadline might coincide with the end of a transition period that probably will have to be granted to the countries that have applied for full membership; i.e., Great Britain, Ireland, Denmark, and Norway.[46]

The Council of Ministers set up a group of high-level experts to study not only the program for economic and monetary union proposed by the EEC Commission, but also other plans aimed at the same objective. Among the latter, the two most important proposals were those by Pierre Werner, the Prime Minister and Finance Minister of Luxembourg, and by Professor Karl Schiller, German Minister of Economics. Werner's plan called for the adoption of a seven-stage program of action, extending over ten years, that would result in the full centralization of European monetary policy. The plan shied away from creating a common European currency, however; this, according to Werner, could only take place after more intensive political integration.[47]

Professor Schiller's plan advocated a realistic procedure
that aimed first at the achievement of the economic and political conditions essential for stable economic development
within the European Community. Then the plan envisaged a
new allocation of powers to the European Community institutions in addition to those provided for by the European Community treaties. Once this had been done and majority decisions had been instituted for the most important fields of
economic, financial, and monetary policies, Professor Schiller
suggested the gradual adoption of a system similar to the
American federal-reserve structure. The culmination of
Professor Schiller's plan would be the creation of a European
monetary unit and the establishment of a Council of European
Central Banks, which would also make decisions by majority
vote. [48]

Without doubt, the achievement of the objectives put forth
in the plans and programs of the EEC Commission, Schiller,
and Werner would be crucial for advancing economic and
political integration in the European Community. It would also
contribute to the solution of those problems that are acutely
plaguing transnational collaboration ventures, such as the
absence of unfettered investment possibilities and the disparities in fiscal legislation of the member states. Interestingly,
in the event of full harmonization of TVA taxes, direct tax
systems and rates would also have to be adjusted. Thus, one
fiscal harmonization measure would engender, if not compel,
other fiscal harmonization measures, a sequence of events
very beneficial for the operations of transnational ventures.

Basically, the plans and programs also reflect the needs
of the member states to avoid currency disturbances of the
kind that took place in 1968 and 1969. The proper functioning
of the common agricultural policy of the Common Market makes
it imperative that currency fluctuations are held to a minimum.
Similarly, the free movement of industrial goods is hampered
by major deviations from traditional currency levels. These
may be some of the reasons that French President Georges
Pompidou lent strong support to the proposals advanced for
the possible creation of a uniform Common Market currency. [49]
Such a new currency would in all likelihood have to be considered as a world-reserve currency and thereby attain a position
similar to that of the American dollar and the British pound
sterling. Although a uniform Common Market currency would
undoubtedly be a step toward a more stable international monetary system, its prospect could also affect the negotiations for
British membership in the EEC, as under these circumstances

the pound sterling may well disappear as a world-reserve currency.

Although these programs and plans will obviously have a far-reaching impact on the international system, putting them into effect will certainly produce serious clashes between those in the national governments anxious to maintain "states rights" and those who are ready to transfer additional powers to the central European Community institutions. In fact, it would not be unreasonable to anticipate that implementation of these programs will develop into an endurance test more serious and searching than any yet experienced in the Common Market.

Although there has been general agreement by the finance ministers on some of the principles to be established in attaining an economic and monetary union, some of the member governments have also expressed various reservations on the suggestion to reduce the present fluctuations during the first stage. One reason is that, although gradual reduction is certainly desirable, it can be achieved only at the same rate at which the medium-term policy objectives are implemented. Moreover, as long as member states pursue different domestic policies in the economic sector, which may result in various rates of inflation, it may be difficult to maintain the objectives of the common economic plans. As a consequence, all member governments must either engage in inflation at the same rate or refrain entirely from using inflation as an economic and political tool within their national frameworks.

In view of the differing political situations in the member states, and in view of national governments' pursuing what they consider favorable electoral prospects, it may not be possible to permit common economic and fiscal policy to take precedence over social and other objectives in individual member states. It is not simply the coordination of economic and monetary policy that is involved, but a very difficult political problem. Given the attitudes of the member governments, as experienced since the late 1950's, and their well-known desire to bargain out national advantages whenever possible in the decisions of the European Community, progress toward economic and monetary union may not go beyond whatever may be the lowest common denominator of national interests.

PREFERRED TACTICS FOR GOAL ATTAINMENT

The preceding discussion of the progress made toward the attainment of the major political objectives pursued by

enterprises involved in transnational collaboration among the
Common Market countries points up several important facts.
It is evident that, despite some progress, these objectives
are far from being reached and that continued efforts are
necessary. In order to obtain favorable responses to the demands articulated by firms engaged in transnational ventures,
a variety of approaches to the EEC system authorities are
taken. Although the central system authorities have been shown
to be generally in favor of the objectives pursued, the subsystem authorities (national administrations, etc.), which
hold key positions in the system's decision-making process,
display varying degrees of reluctance, if not opposition. Therefore, the major efforts have been made on the level of the subsystem authorities, although the central authorities, especially
the EEC Commission, have not been neglected.

It is difficult to determine in detail the methods used by
European companies for the presentation of their demands and
the lobbying efforts undertaken in support of them. European
business executives prefer to conceal such activities as much
as possible and like to claim that they are interested only in
economic matters, not in politics. Nevertheless, from the
interviews and conversations conducted with executives of
collaborating firms and with officials of interest groups, the
national governments, and the European Community, one can
form some impressions of the tactics employed by these firms
for the attainment of their objectives and the successes
achieved.[50]

Coordination of Demands

The special opportunity open to companies engaged in
border-crossing collaboration is the coordination of their demands addressed directly or channeled indirectly to the subsystem authorities. The local partners usually maintain excellent relations with government institutions in their own
countries, providing smooth-flowing transmission belts for
the coordinated demands to the national authorities. The benefits of this coordination can be all the more significant when
collaboration ventures include firms in more than two EEC
countries or when firms such as Farbwerke Hoechst and others
are participating in several of these ventures.

The extent of such coordination can not be fully ascertained,
but there is evidence that it is practiced on a fairly large scale,
although with varying degrees of intensity. When wholly or
jointly owned subsidiaries are small and are located in EEC

countries other than where the company headquarters are,
it is usually considered best to leave them out of the coordination scheme, for under these conditions the political benefits
have proven to be minimal.

On the national level, the previously discussed Fiat/Citroën
affiliation is an excellent example of coordinated effort to obtain government consent for a collaboration agreement. Accord
ing to the press reports cited earlier, François Michelin and
Pierre Bercot, Director-General of Citroën, had relatively
easy access to Prime Minister Maurice Couve de Murville and
other ministers, if not also to President de Gaulle himself.
Moreover, Umberto Agnelli, president of Fiat-France for
several years, had many close acquaintances in French Government circles. All these factors undoubtedly assisted in
reversing within a fortnight the initial French rejection of the
Fiat/Citroën agreement.

Access to the highest organs of government is considered
most rewarding, but approaches to lower government ranks
are also regarded as very important. The previously mentioned
coordinated elaboration and presentation of MAN and Saviem
demands for the equalization of fiscal laws to officials of pertinent German and French ministries is one such example.
The two firms have followed the same procedures with respect
to the harmonization of laws, setting technical standards that
affect the production of trucks. In addition to presenting these
demands to the German and French ministries, the French-
German Committee for Economic and Industrial Cooperation
was tied in with the efforts of the two firms. Although officials
of the two countries have listened sympathetically to these
demands, it is still uncertain whether and what kind of positive
action can be expected on the part of the governments. At the
same time, the EEC Commission is seeking to move forward
on these fronts and the European Parliament is sympathetic,
but the Council of Ministers, beyond approving a general program of the EEC Commission on the equalization of technical
standards, has been dragging its feet.

The interviews and conversations with executives of firms
engaged in transnational collaboration reveal that the MAN and
Saviem lobbying efforts are not isolated cases. In fact, the
various aspects of fiscal harmonization and the equalization of
standards are considered by many executives to be a prime
objective, and a great deal of energy is expanded on attaining
this objective. The pharmaceutical industry, for example,
through its Community Pharmaceutical Industry Group, has
emphasized the need to make strong efforts for the equalization

of legislation in this field and for the harmonization of administrative practices as well. It has also stressed the urgency
of working for the creation of a European patent and has expressed generally its support of the EEC Commission's attempt
to achieve a truly common market in the pharmaceutical
sector.[51]

As far as national interest groups are concerned, there
is a consensus that coordinated demands receive much more
effective backing by specialized groups--for example, associa-
tions of chemical firms--than by the more general organiza-
tions--such as the German BDI or the Federation of Netherlands Industry. The membership of the more general organizations is highly diffuse, which makes it difficult, if not
impossible, to generate concentrated support for demands
favoring only particular industries.

Political parties appear to be employed only to a very
small extent in the channeling of coordinated demands. A
few companies insist on "full orchestration" of their lobbying
efforts, however, and it may be assumed that these efforts
include parties in EEC countries where they have a measure
of effectiveness in influencing the government decision-making
process.

On the European level, the more than 300 specialized confederations are also considered more potent to press coordinated demands of collaborating firms than UNICE is, although
the effectiveness of these confederations varies widely.
(Some of the confederations seem to provide mainly a center
for entertainment for visitors from the national groups and
accomplish very little serious work.) The main task of the
confederations is to ensure that these demands become official
proposals of the EEC Commission. For example, the European Federation of Mechanical and Metalworking Industries
has approached the EEC Commission in order to urge liberal
interpretation of the European Community antitrust laws for
collaborating ventures even if they constitute a certain restric-
tion of free competition.[52]

Beyond contacts with the EEC Commissioners, the confederation staff also seeks access to middle-rank EEC officials,
in order to get advance information on EEC Commission proposals and to influence their development. From time to time,
visits are also scheduled with members of the Economic and
Social Committee and the Committee of Permanent Representatives to pursue similar purposes.

In a few cases, collaborating firms have established their
own liaison bureaus in Brussels, and some large corporations

like Fiat or Shell maintain either their exclusive offices or
permanent representatives in that city. Their basic functions
are more or less the same as those performed by the confederations, but they are able to provide more individual treatmen
for the demands of their principals, thereby enhancing in some
instances the potential for success. The Fiat office is headed
by a former Italian ambassador, who enjoys direct access to
the members of the EEC Commission and other high Commissic
officials.[53] Below him is a Fiat staff officer who contacts the
middle-rank EEC Commission officials (from director down)
and other EEC institutions. He also has close relations with
the Italian Permanent Mission to the Communities and occasionally deals with UNICE, although that relationship is maintained mainly through Confindustria, the national Italian
federation of industry.

Style of Demands

In order to achieve their objectives, the enterprises concerned are likely to use a variety of means--from subtle
influences to potent pressures. They may seek to persuade
government officials and perhaps even the public that the attainment of these objectives is "good for the government and the
country." They may occasionally conceal some of the things
that they are doing because of obvious misgivings of public
officials. Finally, they may endeavor to enlist the government
machinery and the economic power of the parent government
to compel acceptance of their objectives by the foreign government.

When presenting coordinated demands, however, they
generally avoid aggressiveness in content and form. Rather,
the demands are couched in more or less academic language,
and a climate of restraint and objectivity is regarded as beneficial for their discussion. In other words, no obvious and
strong political pressures are used in the pursuit of this type
of demand.

EFFECTS ON POLITICAL INTEGRATION

Question was raised in Chapter 1 about the contribution
that transnational business collaboration could make to the
process of political integration. Despite the weakness of the

statistical data presented in Chapter 2, they reveal that a substantial and increasing number of enterprises in two or more
EEC countries are engaged in border-crossing collaboration,
although the emerging network of transnational interlacement
is not entirely symmetric in terms of national participation.
The results of this expanding network--such as the increasing
use of the economies of scale where feasible and advantageous,
the technological improvements resulting from research made
possible by cost-sharing, the enhancement of competitiveness
in the enlarged market because of greater marketing efficiency
and reduced production costs, and the more efficient utilization
of resources--can be seen as some of the indicators that economic integration in the Common Market is proceeding successfully.[54] Another indicator would be an increase in economic
growth.

Although "measures designed to abolish discrimination
between economic units belonging to different states"[55] were
essential for initiating the process of economic integration,
the national economies are now beginning to "grow together,"[56]
and border-crossing collaboration ventures play an important
part in this movement. But, as has been seen, the smooth
functioning of these ventures is being impeded by a number of
government-related obstacles. As a consequence, demands
have been generated for the attainment of several major political objectives to secure optimal conditions for the operations
of transnational business collaboration in the EEC.

To assess the effects of the preceding developments upon
the process of political integration, some criteria are necessary
to gauge the progress of this process. In his conceptualization
of the EEC as an incipient political system, Lindberg has
suggested several indices for measuring political integration,
which, in a somewhat simplified and modified form, appear
to be applicable here. One index pertains to the extent of
political community and is based on a seven-point scale of
decisional locus:

(1) Decisions are taken entirely in the European
Community system.

(2) Decisions are taken almost entirely in the
European Community system.

(3) Decisions are taken predominately in the
European Community system, but the nation-states
play a significant role in decision-making.

(4) Decisions are taken about equally in the
European Community system and the nation-states.

(5) Decisions are taken predominately by the
nation-states, but the European Community system
plays a significant role in decision-making.
(6) Decisions are taken almost entirely by the
nation-states.
(7) Decisions are taken entirely by the nation-
states individually. [57]

A second index, related to the first, concerns the saliency
of the issue or functional areas in which decisions might be
taken under varying degrees of political division of labor between the European Community system and the national system.
The more the EEC system is enabled to allocate values "that
are perceived as highly significant by the members of the
society," the more intense their desire to work together in
a common division of labor is likely to be. [58] Moreover, the
ability of the EEC to allocate values perceived as important
by most of its members is, according to Lindberg, a sign
that the system has considerable stress-responding capabilities
because support for the EEC as a political community would
be extensive.

The degree of saliency of an issue area depends on how
large a segment of the society is affected by the allocation of
values, how important they are to the members' welfare, and
how politically powerful their position is in society. Further-
more, the saliency is enhanced when the pertinent decisions
taken by the EEC system affect national subsystems in relation
to each other and to the European Community. [59] A scale
ranging from low, through moderate, to high saliency could
be applied for rough measurement.

A third useful index pertains to "the relative ability of
the subsystem authorities acting unilaterally or collectively
(in the Council) and the system authorities, especially the
Commission, to dominate or overawe each other in the Community political process." [60] A five-point scale ranging from
peripheralization to centralization suggests various possibilities
and reflects increased (or diminished) input of support for the
system authorities:

(1) subsystem authorities can unilaterally
overawe system authorities and other subsystem
authorities (de Gaulle's veto power);
(2) subsystem authorities can collectively
overawe system authorities (Council of Ministers
refuses to pass proposals of EEC Commission or
does so only after very substantial modification);

(3) subsystem authorities cannot overawe but
can significantly vary the behavior of system authorities;
(4) system authorities cannot overawe but can
delimit the activities of subsystem authorities and
keep its own decisions from being overruled; and
(5) system authorities can completely overawe
subsystem authorities.[61]

Basically, support refers to the attitudes of the masses and
elites, especially those politically powerful, toward an environment conducive to the operation of a collective decision-making
process, as prescribed by the EEC treaty and evolved in
practice in the form of bargaining, negotiation, and consultation.
Intense support would involve a commitment to a "European"
ideology and concomitant values, implying a high priority for
the assignment of additional functions to the system authorities, as well as for the eventual creation of a united Europe.

In summary then, high integration would create conditions
under which decisions on all or the most important functions
were made in the European Community system, the procedures
for that system were fully accepted and aspirations were
apparent for the assignment of additional functions to the system, and the ability of the subsystem authorities to dominate
the system authorities were therefore limited or nonexistent.

In this assessment of the effects of transnational business
collaboration on the process of political integration, the working
hypothesis will be that the spreading net of border-crossing
collaboration generates pressures for the attainment of certain
political objectives and that the more successful the attainment
of these objectives, the higher the level of political integration
is likely to be. The application of the three indices delineated
above will help determine in rather crude form the extent, if
any, to which political integration has advanced or the conditions under which it might advance.

If the first five political objectives of collaborating firms
outlined earlier (See p. 66 .) were attained, the autonomy of
the member states to take decisions would be reduced implicitly, if not explicitly, producing a corresponding increase in
the power of central European Community authorities. As
far as the sixth objective--the liberal application of the EEC
antitrust laws--is concerned, little change in the distribution
of decisional powers would be caused by its attainment, unless
it led to an equalization of national and European Community
antitrust laws or to the recognized dominance of the European

Community laws. In any case, attainment of the above objectives would signify a general shift of the decisional locus in important policy areas toward the central authorities of the European Community system and, according to Lindberg's scale (See pp. 82-83, above.), it would be justified to state that pertinent decisions would be taken "equally in the European Community and the nation-states." The same considerations would also apply in the event of full institutionalized coordination of economic and monetary policies.

But the shift of the decisional locus is only one criterion by which to gauge the potential impact of transnational business collaboration on the process of political integration. The second, closely related, criterion is its saliency for this process. In the application of the concept of saliency here, it is necessary to recognize first that, although some of the largest enterprises in the EEC are participating in transnational ventures, the total number of these ventures is relatively small when compared with the total number of business enterprises existing in the EEC countries. Yet the benefits from the attainment of their major objectives would flow not only to the collaborating enterprises, but also to thousands of other firms in the Common Market. In other words, the collaborating enterprises would have acted as something of a special shock force for the good of much of the EEC business community, and the resulting allocation of values would be perceived as important by an appreciable number of system members.

One could also argue that, in addition to the cost reductions produced by border-crossing collaboration ventures themselves, the elimination of border customs check points and the harmonization of fiscal and other laws are likely to bring about further savings in the cost of production and marketing, which would be passed on to the consumers in the form of lower prices. Thus, the circle of persons benefiting from the allocated values would be greatly enlarged and the saliency of the issue area would become more pronounced.

Whether production cost savings would lead to price reductions, however, is not certain. Some doubt arises because of the insistence of the collaborating firms on a liberal application of the European Community antitrust provisions. Moreover, certain European studies of industrial concentration, where cost savings might be expected, suggest that no correlation exists between increased industrial concentration and the formation of prices; however, these studies disclose a positive correlation between the degree of industrial concentration and the payment of higher wages.[62] As a consequence, one could

expect an enlargement of the circle of system members who
would benefit from the allocation of values as the result of
improved conditions for border-crossing collaborations and
for whose welfare this allocation would be very important.
(The number of employees of fifteen EEC-based enterprises
engaged in transnational ventures of different types that are
listed among the fifty largest corporations outside the United
States totals a respectable 2,074,931. [63] The total civilian
labor force in the EEC is approximately 74 million.)

A rise in the saliency of the issue area under study may
be caused also by the continuous transactional flows between
collaborating firms and the necessary interaction of the management and technical staffs. As discussed earlier, the coordination of the joint activities is usually carried out through a network of committees and working groups composed of an equal
number of officials from the collaborating firms. (See pp. 32-
34 and 43-45, above.) Depending on the size of the firms and
the range of the joint activities, fifty to 200 officials may be
involved in the coordinating operations.

Although frictions and frustrations are not infrequent,
especially because of diverging viewpoints on technical matters,
a feeling of belonging to a group with shared goals develops,
which eases communications among the individuals involved
and sometimes leads to close personal relationships. Because
many members of this group perceive their activities as related to the framework of the Common Market, the subtle
operation of a political socialization process among them has
been noted and, as a result, an increased identification with
European values and ideologies, as well as, perhaps, a
gradually deepening commitment to European Community
norms of conduct.

This group, which is bound to grow in members as the
number of joint transnational ventures expands, may develop
into a special type of Europe-oriented business elite whose
future behavior will be of consequence to the functioning of
the political systems in which they live. Since many members
of this group are relatively young, their positions of power
are likely to be still on the rise, and therefore their outlook
and influence may in time further enhance the saliency of
transnational collaboration for the process of political integration.

As stated earlier, the saliency of an issue area rises
when it affects the relations between the European Community
and the subsystems, and especially those among the subsystems
themselves. Clearly, transnational business collaboration

affects these relations, especially when one considers the
implications for conflict inherent in the pursuit and eventual
attainment of the objectives of collaborating firms. Considering all factors, it seems justified to assign to transnational
business collaboration a saliency score of at least "moderate."

So far, this analysis has been largely concerned with the
potential effect of transnational business collaboration on
political integration. From the discussion of the objectives
of collaborating firms it is clear that progress in their attainment has up to now been spotty and slow. The peripheralization-centralization index is closely linked to the degree of
support tendered to the European Community system, and it
is the degree of this support on the part of the politically
powerful elites that can be assumed to be a major factor for
progress in the attainment of these objectives.

The nationalistic orientation of the member governments
has been alluded to several times, as has their strong penchant
for continued autonomy, despite repeated broad declarations
over the years by at least five of these governments that they
strongly favor European unification. Specific examples were
the attitude of the French Government toward the Fiat/Citroën
agreement and that of the German Government toward the
attempted CFP participation in the GBAG. Another example
involves the Italian Government, which in 1968 imposed a
national solution for collaboration on the chemical industry
when it permitted the state-controlled ENI and IRI conglomer-
ates to take control of Italy's foremost chemical enterprise,
the privately owned Montecatini-Edison group. This effectively
prevented any possible transnational collaboration of
Montecatini-Edison with chemical companies of other EEC
countries, which could have been used for the infusion of needed
new capital and the improvement of its deteriorating competitive
position. The action of the Italian Government instituted, in
fact, a national monopoly in the chemical industry, and the new
organization now represents the largest chemical unit within
the Common Market.[64] (Private shareholders of Montecatini-
Edison continue to oppose the take-over, but with only limited
success.[65])

LAGGING SUPPORT FOR
EUROPEAN COMMUNITY SYSTEM

National Bureaucracies

The low level of support for the European Community
system suggested by these actions and other manifestations of
national preference on the part of the EEC member governments stems in part from the attitudes of many civil servants
in the national ministries. As pointed out earlier, these people
exercise far-reaching gatekeeping functions in the European
Community system. (See pp. 59-60, above.) The attitude of
national civil servants is highly complex and should be a fruitful field for further research. Officials in the EEC countries,
except France and Italy, with whom the author had conversations stressed at first their support for European unification.
But later in the conversations a variety of reservations and
objections appeared, which almost reversed their first views.

Motivated, perhaps unconsciously, by the fear of reduced
functions, with a corresponding loss of their positions of power,
in a Europe where the important decisions would be made on
a higher level than the national plane, they seem to be in no
hurry to move the coordinating and harmonizing activities in
the EEC forward. As the technical experts in the preparation
of legislative and administrative proposals, they can find many
reasons why the coordination of certain policies or the harmonization of specific laws should be delayed. Moreover, the
status quo is always easier to defend than are reasons for
innovations. [66]

Even if some members of the national parliaments were
really enthusiastic and willing to push through needed legislation
that would aid the integration process in the Common Market,
they usually do not possess the necessary staff nor the expert
knowledge to prepare the required legislative proposals. Thus,
they are at the mercy of the national bureaucrats, who, if they
want to, can easily and subtly sabotage the wishes of the legis-
lators. With respect to these problems, Franz-Josef Strauss,
the West Berman Minister of Finance and a man who should
know, made the following significant comments:

> sometimes shortsighted ambition of nationalisti-
> cally oriented bureaucracies as well as lack of
> decisiveness on the part of responsible politicians
> leads to an overgrowth of egocentric interests. We

observe not without apprehension that after the dismantlement of the tariff walls new national paper
walls are being erected surreptitiously through the
issuance of drawn-out indeterminable regulations.
The re-nationalization of ideas is followed by the
re-nationalization of secret bureaucratic decisions.
With the slogan of the sovereignty of the states and
the pursuit of their own interests, it is quite easy
to manipulate [the bureaucratic schemes] .[67]

The attitudes of the national bureaucracies should really
not be surprising for several reasons. First, as Downs points
out, the behavior of officials is motivated significantly by re-
numeration, security, prestige, and considerations of power
within and outside their specific functional areas.[68] Although
they are committed to serve the public interest, their private
motives tend to color their perceptions as to what this interest
is. Neither these perceptions nor their norms of conduct can
be readily changed by the political leadership. Max Weber,
in his study of bureaucracy, stressed that large, long-establish
state bureaucracies are capable of considerable independence
and insulation from the political leadership and are far from
being passive tools of those who yield political power in a
state.[69]
     Second, all officials tend to oppose changes that decrease
the number, scope, or relative importance of the functions
entrusted to them. Like most large organizations, administrative institutions have a powerful propensity to continue doing
today whatever they did yesterday. The main reason for this
inertia is that established processes represent an enormous
previous investment in time, effort, and money. Moreover,
it took a significant investment to build up the number of
officials necessary for running the institution and to develop
its clientele, which, in time, accepted and became used to the
behavior pattern of the institution. To justify its continued
existence, every institution wants to retain its clientele and,
for this reason, cherishes its relations with the members of
this group. As a consequence, significant changes will be
strongly resisted, and the larger the number of officials
affected, the greater will be the resistance. This reluctance
to change is reinforced by self-interest, which contributed
much to the motivation of the behavior of civil servants.[70]
In this connection it is interesting to note that Belgian officials
still refuse to accept the fact that Gevaerts has become a
"transnational" company through its affiliation with Agfa and

continue to insist on treating it as an exclusively Belgian
enterprise.

To carry out major changes in institutional tasks successfully may, therefore, require compensation to officials affected
by the loss of functions in the form of offsetting benefits and
incentives. The failure to "sweeten" proposals for change
will result in tensions and is apt to produce subtle sabotage
of the proposed changes, as noted above with respect to the
political objectives of transnational ventures. For these
reasons compensatory schemes need to be worked up in order
to promote acceptance of the transfer of functions from the
national to the European level by the national civil servants
adversely affected. (It is interesting to note that, when, as
the result of the implementation of the European Community's
common agricultural policy, certain functions regarding price
formation had to be transferred from the national ministries
to the EEC institutions, the German federal authorities were
compelled to share part of the remaining functions in the farm
structure field with the state authorities in order to assuage
the opposition of the latter to a complete loss of their functions
in this area.)

The elaboration of such schemes will tax the imagination
of the national leadership in the member states. If a forward
movement in the process of political integration is sincerely
desired, however, the necessary support of the European
Community system by the national bureaucracies must be
generated. For this reason these schemes seem to be essential.

Influence of European Civil Service

In connection with these schemes, the relationship between
the European Community civil service and the national bureaucracies must be examined. The salary scales of the former
are higher than those of the latter; in addition, European
Community officials benefit from much lower tax rates and
certain diplomatic immunities. [71] The psychological consequences of this imbalance are often a feeling of superiority
on the part of the European Community officials and sentiments
of animosity and envy on the part of the national civil servants.

Another aspect of the relationship between the European
Community and the national civil services is a subtle political
and bureaucratic socialization process toward the adoption of
European values, beliefs, and norms of conduct among national

civil servants. This process occurs under certain conditions
and is strongly resisted by the majority of the national administrative elites. It operates among several groups of national
civil servants active in various phases of European Community
decision-making, with the European Community civil servants
acting as "socializing agents."

One group consists of the staff members of the permanent
diplomatic missions of the member states in Brussels. These
officials are known to have frequently adopted a more "European" than strictly national orientation in the perception of
what is best for the pursuit of their governments' objectives.
This fledgling "European" orientation has been frowned upon
in most cases in the national ministries and has, in fact, at
times provoked hostile, counterproductive reactions rather
than sympathetic consent.

The second group includes thousands of national civil
servants who are called to Brussels on various occasions for
expert consultation by the EEC Commission, the Council of
Ministers, and other EEC bodies. These consultations on
EEC problems expose them to the socialization process, but
the long-range effects appear to be minimal.

The third group is composed of officials who perhaps had
been attracted by the higher pay to leave the national civil
services and to seek employment in the EEC, but who for a
variety of reasons later returned to their own civil service.
If their return was motivated by disillusionment with the
European Community system, the effects of the socialization
process, whatever they might have been, are likely to have
been erased.

If their original transfer to the European Community
civil service had been prompted by acquiring experiences that
they hoped to use for promotion in their own civil services,
however, they may seek to spread their newly adopted European ideologies in their national civil services. (It is interesting to note that French officials that have been assigned to
duties with the French mission to the EEC receive promotions
upon their return to France. Whether this policy also applies
to individuals who have entered the European Community civil
service and transfer back to the French service is not clear.
Former national officials that have moved to the European
Community sometimes attempt to bargain out promotions in
the national civil service prior to returning.) This may be the
case particularly if they are assigned to administrative divisions dealing with EEC matters. (In Germany there appears
to be an increasing interest among younger civil servants for

assignment to these divisions, which is perhaps a sign of
beginning change. It is perhaps significant, however, that,
during a simulation exercise on European integration carried
out by younger German officials during a special training course,
emphasis was placed more on the preservation of national
interests than on the definition and emergence of a true European Community interest.)

Upon their return, however, they will also be exposed
again to the bureaucratic ideologies of their own national civil
services, which will emphasize the benefits that are likely to
accrue to large numbers of citizens from the efficiency of the
institutions to which they are assigned. As Downs points out,
bureaucratic ideologies will almost invariably seek to maintain
or expand the activities of existing administrative institutions
rather than see them contracted. When other agencies, such
as perhaps those of the EEC, are trying to capture the functions
of an existing institution of a member state, its ideology will
demarcate sharply the borders of its proper activities and
claim that the "invading agencies" are "beyond the legitimate
bounds of their logical functions."[72]

The foregoing brief discussion of certain aspects of the
interrelationship between the European Community and national
civil services appears to strengthen the proposition that compensatory schemes are needed if favorable attitudes toward
strong support of the European Community system and its
procedures are to be developed among the national bureaucracies, especially among the top layers. The success of
these schemes may depend to a considerable degree on the
attitudes of the political elites, particularly those elected to
office, as they may claim to represent the wishes of their con-
stituents regarding European Community support.

Role of Political Parties

Most of the political parties in the EEC countries emphasize in their programs varying degrees of support for European
unification. In fact, the parliamentary party of the CDU/CSU
has specifically demanded the coordination of economic and
fiscal policies and the harmonization of the appropriate laws.[73]
But studies made on the role that European questions have
actually played in elections (the Netherlands elections in 1967
and the West German elections in 1965) suggest that these
questions aroused little interest and that their impact on voter
motivation was minimal.[74] A somewhat different situation

existed during the French presidential elections in 1965, when
the Common Market crisis provoked by de Gaulle's boycott of
European Community proceedings caused serious apprehension
among the French farmers about the future of the Common
Agricultural Policy (CAP) and thereby raised the level of interest in European questions. Nevertheless, it was the consensus of the persons interviewed by the author that, in the
election of a candidate to political office, his support for
political unification had practically no influence on the outcome
of his election.

This should not be taken to signify that the majorities of
the electorates in the EEC countries are "anti-European," but
simply that other issues are decisive.[75] Although a majority
of the public in the member states is in favor of the European
Community and European union, the opinions expressed suggest
a rather nebulous sensitivity to European problems and only
vague knowledge. Equally vague are the motiviations for the
favorable attitudes. Certainly, the strong backing of European
unity prominently displayed in the election program of French
presidential candidate Alain Poher, announced six days before
the first election run in 1969, did not gain him additional votes;
in fact, his percentage of votes received during this election
run was substantially lower than that indicated in the public-
opinion polls taken just prior to the announcement, although
no causality between the announcement and the poor election
result can be assumed.[76]

Under these circumstances, the backing expressed by the
party programs for political integration seems to have a hollow
ring, and few effective pressures may be expected to be exerted
on the national administrations to increase their support for the
European Community system values and operating procedures.
A number of new parties dedicated chiefly to European unification have sprung up during the late 1960's, but they have
been able to attract only a tiny number of voters.[77] (In the
West German elections of September, 1969, for example, the
Europa Partei received less than 0.5 per cent of the votes
cast.[78])

Parliamentary deputies are only infrequently urged by
firms engaged in transnational collaboration ventures to press
their demands energetically, for those firms do not use party
channels often for the promotion of demands. Conversely,
small businessmen who frequently regard transnational collaboration coupled with industrial concentration as a threat to their
survival and for whom the national markets remain the proper
framework for their activities, request protection, sometimes

vociferously, in parliamentary committees, professional
organizations, and from the national governmental agencies. [79]
Such manifestations are caution signals for the political parties
and reinforce the low support dispositions of the national administrations.

Labor Unions: Conflicting Interests

The attitudes toward the European Community system of
another group of political actors, the labor unions, although
they are on the surface basically favorable, are complex and
have, in fact, been influenced by the spread of transnational
business collaboration. The concern of labor about the possible
loss of jobs and about the uncontrolled outflow of national capital resulting from joint ventures has already been mentioned
in the discussion of the Fiat/Citroën agreement. Their critical
positions toward the project of a "European" company statute
have also been pointed out. Some of the unions, especially
those on the left, also have ideological grounds for their opposition to transnational business ventures. In their opinion,
these may result in capitalistic monopolies entirely devoid of
any state control. [80]

A somewhat similar, but more moderate, note has been
struck by the International Confederation of Free Trade Unions
(ICFTU) during its world congress in July, 1969. In the opinion
of the ICFTU, multinational companies and, implicitly, transnational business collaboration represent new challenge to the
trade-union movement, particularly since they are able to
transfer production units and research centers arbitrarily from
one country to another, to jeopardize democratic national
planning, and to evade national taxes. A resolution passed by
the ICFTU congress stressed the need to set up adequate
national measures to control multinational companies and to
"democratize" them. [81] The Free Work World, monthly pub-
lication of the ICFTU, followed up on the resolution by stres-
sing in its July-August, 1969, issue that the first task of the
unions was to exert pressures for strict enforcement of the
national antitrust and company laws in order to prevent the
giants of the industrial world from abusing their enormous
power. [82]

Although these concerns and fears tend to lower the unions'
support level for the European Community systems, they may
also stimulate the pursuit of certain objectives that might
strengthen this support. In response to expanding transnational

collaboration by business enterprises, the unions have been
spurred to turn their attention increasingly to transnational
bargaining in order to "level up" labor's benefits. Heinz O.
Vetter, the chairman of the German Federation of Trade Unions
(DGB), after declaring that "the industrial giants which reach
beyond national borders will ruthlessly exploit the international
working cost differential for the purpose of increasing their
profit," stated:

> We must, therefore, see to it that the international
> combines will in the future conclude collective agree-
> ments on wage, working conditions, and social bene-
> fits on the basis of coordinated collective bargaining
> with the trade unions. The [DGB] will do its utmost
> within . . . the recently founded European Federation
> of Free Trade Unions . . . to promote fulfillment of
> this challenge.[83]

Although it is most likely difficult to bargain at present on
a European Community-wide basis with respect to wages, because the social legislation in the member states varies widely
and social benefits and charges, therefore, differ from country
to country, the unions have already begun to meet with employers in the Common Market to discuss the harmonization of
working conditions and retraining programs across national
boundaries. For example, a meeting was held in 1967 between
the European Committee of the Christian Metal Workers'
Unions, joined by other international organizations of the same
union, and management staff members of Philips. The topics
of the meeting also included labor costs in the EEC and the
effect of automation and production rationalization on labor.
The Socialist labor unions also held a meeting with the Philips
management, in 1969, during which similar topics were discussed.[84] In this connection, it is noteworthy that the Italian
and French unions representing the workers of the Fiat and
Citroën enterprises, including the Communist-controlled unions
but excluding the Force Ouvrière, have organized joint meetings
to work out common strategies for dealing with the management
of the collaborating firms.

New pressures to raise the European Community support
level of the national administrations may also come from the
newly rebuilt and expanded European organizations of the
Christian and Socialist unions in the EEC countries. (The
organization of the Christian unions, formerly the CISC, is
now called l'Organisation Européenne de la Confédération

Mondiale du Travail. The counterpart of the Socialist unions,
formerly CISL, is now the Confédération Européenne des
Syndicats Libres dans la Communauté.)[85] In their strongly
pro-integrationist programs these groups list as specific goals
the bargaining with employers on a Common Market-wide
basis. A first Common Market-wide bargaining agreement
was concluded in 1968 between COPA (Comité des Organisations
Professionelles Agricoles de la CEE) and the Christian and
Socialist union confederations; it covers the working hours
and rest periods for salaried agricultural workers.[86] Other
similar projects are now under study by the unions.

Political Influence of Business Elites

One may wonder why the business elites interested in
obtaining optimal conditions for transnational ventures have
not been able to raise the support level for the European Community system sufficiently to speed up the successful pursuit
of their political objectives. As the previous discussion of
the presentation of demands by collaborating firms indicated,
strong pressures and bluntness are avoided. In addition, these
demands clearly fall into the category of what Ernst B. Haas
calls "pragmatic-interest politics." The interests pursued
are pragmatic and generally not reinforced with deep ideological
or philosophical commitment.

Although many top-level executives in enterprises engaged
in transnational collaboration are committed to European values
and the European Community system, they are not prepared
to man the ramparts for European political unity. Rather, they
accept gradual, incremental progress and seek to obtain their
goals through persistant, but undramatic, efforts. Thus, the
pursuit of their objectives can be slowed down or halted without
too much difficulty. As Haas has pointed out, "a political
process that is built and projected from pragmatic interests,
. . . is bound to be a frail process susceptible to reversal."[87]
(A few leaders of transnational ventures, such as Giovanni
Agnelli of Fiat, have displayed strong ideological commitment
to European unification. In a speech in New York in January,
1969, Agnelli advocated "a gigantic transfer of political power
from the national to the European level."[88])

Moreover, the reluctance of the national bureaucracies to
move ahead promptly with legal harmonization and policy
coordination not only is related to the pursuit of their own
vested interests, but is often buttressed by a strong nationalistic ideology. The same may be said of the fears of small

businessmen in the EEC to accept the Common Market as the proper framework for their business activities. This and the other factors discussed above seem to be largely responsible for the slow progress made so far by those who would like to see the political obstacles to the effective functioning of trans- national business collaboration removed as quickly as possible.

Although the summit conference at The Hague in December, 1969, created a new atmosphere and spirit conducive to further integration, the concrete advances made in the areas of special interest and concern to collaborating entities as a result of the conference have remained small. The vista has brightened, however; the fact that the European Community will be permitted progressively to have its own financial resources--the European Parliament will share control over them by 1975 with the Council of Ministers[89] --may suggest gradual changes in the support for the European Community by politically power- ful elites. But the depth of these changes in favor of European Community support cannot yet be fully determined. They may become apparent when the national parliaments of the EEC member states debate the ratification of the agreement amend- ing the European Community treaties in order to institute the new system of financial resources.

It is perhaps symptomatic of the continuing concern with national prerogatives and it confirms previous experiences that, shortly after the text of this amendment was drawn up, arguments arose over the interpretation of the scope of the powers to be exercised by the European Parliament in 1975. The Council of Ministers did not accept the extensive inter- pretation advanced by the European Parliament and only pro- mised to re-examine the situation in 1972 in the light of the ratification debates in the national parliaments, the over-all development of the European Community, and the institutional problems raised by the enlargement of the European Commun- ity.[90]

All this suggests that an evaluation of present European Community support must remain cautious.[91] Under the peripheralization-centralization scale outlined above (See p. 83) current conditions may be characterized best as subsystem (national) authorities can collectively overawe system authori- ties. This also means that, until the support levels of politi- cally powerful elites are raised substantially, progress in the attainment of the political objectives is likely to be slow and the decisional locus probably will not shift beyond the stage where decisions are taken predominantly by the nation-states, but the European Community system plays a significant role in the decision-making process.

POSSIBLE FUTURE EFFECTS ON
POLITICAL INTEGRATION

As far as the current situation is concerned, although the contribution of transnational business collaboration to the process of political integration cannot be regarded as very auspicious, certain by-products of this collaboration clearly have favorable implications for the future. Increasing numbers of firms and persons have a stake in the harmonization measures and other objectives of collaborating enterprises as direct or indirect beneficiaries and, as pertinent harmonization measures are instituted, many of them are likely to perceive the continuation of these measures as vested interests. They therefore constitute an increasingly powerful force that, if it could be fully mobilized, would, at a minimum, strongly resist attempts to lower the level of political integration again by reinstituting the full autonomy of the member governments in the fiscal and other areas of concern.

If such attempts were made, they may well develop into domestic political issues in the member states, similar to those raised by the French farmers in 1965 following de Gaulle's boycott of the EEC institutions. As a consequence, the European question may assume greater significance in the outcome of forthcoming elections, which, in turn, might create a greater interest by elected political elites in integration and the European Community system and might elicit more genuine support for its institutions, procedures, and norms of conduct.

Another by-product with potentially favorable implications for political integration is the gradual emergence of an expanding, relatively young, Europe-oriented business elite as the result of the subtle political socialization process operative in the coordinating mechanisms of collaborating entities. Although it is impossible to determine the precise effect of this elite on the progress of political integration, it is obvious that its members are also likely to feel a vested interest in the maintenance of the integration level achieved. But, more importantly, the members of the elite may be influential through intracountry and transnational cross communication with other elites in soliciting increased support for harmonization measures by the member governments, as well as for the Community system in general, and may thereby evolve as a significant pro-integration force.

Finally, the unions in the member states may eventually emerge as potent, although perhaps reluctant, allies in the

pursuit of the objectives sought by enterprises engaged in
transnational collaboration. Since improved operating conditions for transnational ventures may lead to higher wages
and better working conditions, the unions should recognize
that their interests may well converge with those of border-
crossing business entities. In addition, the eventual harmonization of social legislation, which undoubtedly would serve
the long-range interests of labor, may be achieved with greater
ease when considered as a natural sequel to the harmonization
measures sought by transnational business collaboration.
Therefore, a coalition between a Europe-oriented business elite
and a less parochially oriented labor elite would not be inconceivable and would most likely constitute a powerful force for
gathering support for the European Community system and
for overcoming the nationalistic tendencies of many political
and administrative elites.

Proposal for Common Industrial Policy

The EEC Commission is fully aware of the contribution
that transnational business collaboration can make to the
process of integration. At the same time, it recognizes that
national collaborations and mergers tend to harm this process
In April, 1970, the EEC Commission published a memorandum
on a proposed European Community industrial policy that analyzes the political, legal, and psychological barriers to transnational amalgamations and stresses the urgent need for more
border-crossing ventures in the Common Market.[92] The
memorandum points out that productivity per worker in the
Common Market in 1968 was nearly 40 per cent below that of
an American worker and that average wages were more than
40 per cent below that of American labor.

According to the EEC Commission, only the elaboration
and acceptance of a common industrial development policy can
ensure the full vitality of Europe's industrial posture, sus-
tained economic expansion, and a reasonable amount of technological independence from other world powers, i.e., mainly
the United States. At the same time, such a policy would
create the irreversible preconditions for Western Europe's
economic unity and later for its political unification.[93]

The memorandum pursues several basic targets. Highest
priority seems to have been accorded to the completion of a
truly single market in the European Community. For this
reason, it deplores the very slow progress being made in the

harmonization of technical standards despite the fact that the
Council of Ministers has adopted a general harmonization program in this field. Another impediment to the completion of
a unified market focused upon by the memorandum is the practice of national authorities to reserve public contracts to
national enterprises in their own countries. The EEC Commission points out that these practices have been illegal since
January 1, 1970, but they continue nevertheless. The industrial sectors especially affected are capital-goods manufacturers and industries producing technologically advanced
equipment. For the latter firms, public contracts represent
a major outlet; as a result of the national purchasing practices,
de facto fragmentation remains the rule in these industries,
although, in view of very high research and development costs,
transnational collaboration and consolidation should be sought.
The EEC Commission intends to publish statistics to show
which governments are bestowing public contracts to firms
other than those located in their own country and to submit
proposals to the Council of Ministers that, if adopted, would
eventually halt the illegal practices.

    The second target of the EEC Commission memorandum
is the unification of the fiscal, financial, and legal frameworks
under which firms in the European Community must operate.
It exhorts the member governments to speed up the process of
unification, as otherwise industry cannot draw all the benefits
that it is entitled to expect from the existence of the European
Community. In particular, the EEC Commission is anxious
that work on the statute for a European company be resumed
and hopes for adoption with the least possible delay. Moreover, it also seeks to explore common legal forms for other
structures, such as the company with limited liability, frequently used in Germany, and the French groupement d'intérèt
économique.

    The third target of the memorandum involves changes in
the structure and organization of firms. The EEC Commission
stresses that the relative lag in Europe's industrial development and the keen competition from firms outside the European
Community make the creation of transnational affiliations among
EEC companies essential and urgent, particularly in the technologically advanced industries. A higher degree of concentration is therefore needed, which should be allowed provided
competition is not unduly restrained. To this end, the EEC
Commission urges the member governments to adopt a favorable
attitude and to refrain from opposing transnational amalgamations.

In order to provide financial assistance to companies located in different member states that are interested in trans national collaboration, the EEC Commission considers the European Investment Bank to be an immediate resource. It has also decided to utilize for this purpose funds accruing to it under the system of tax levies authorized by Articles 49-51 of the European Coal and Steel Treaty. Additional funds to meet the financial needs of companies contemplating border-crossing collaboration may become available when the European Community as a whole has its own financial resources. Precise allocations for this purpose, however, may depend not so much on the will and decisions of the EEC Commission, but on the actual balance drawn between the budgetary powers of the Council of Ministers and the European Parliament. Moreover, the statute of the European Investment Bank may have to be revised before the proposed actions can be taken.

Finally, the EEC Commission is exploring the possibility of setting up a European Community-wide coordinating office that would award European Community development contracts, particularly in the field of advanced technology. For the awar of these contracts, which would be financed from the European Community's own resources, priority would be given to companies that have decided to engage in transnational collaboration and restructuring.

The fourth target of the EEC Commission memorandum is the organization of social and economic change. The EEC Commission recognizes that transnational business collaboration and amalgamations have already produced changes in the pattern of employment and that this process of change is likely to become more acute in the years to come. As a consequence many workers will have to change jobs, and some will have to undergo retraining; however, working conditions may well be improved, wage levels may be raised, and skills of large numbers of workers may be refined.

The EEC Commission believes that a highly energetic and wideranging policy is needed to reduce the painful effects of the changes that will be encountered and suggests that planned reforms of the European Social Fund be shaped in such a way as to permit financial contributions for this purpose. With respect to management personnel, the EEC Commission calls on European Community firms to take the initiative in establishing and financing a European Management and Training Foundation. Such an organization would be able to provide a center, closely linked with universities and specialized institutes, where modern management techniques would be studied. It could also act as a breeding ground for management specialists for industry, considering the special knowledge necessary for the operations of transnational ventures.

The memorandum of the EEC Commission represents more than the definition of a new common policy. Rather, it constitutes a guide for an over-all offensive strategy whose various parts can be applied to numerous fields of European Community and national activity. Specific actions are advocated for the present and a broad picture is painted for the future. Although the memorandum is clearly designed to prod the national governments to expedite legal and policy harmonization measures, it also looks beyond the confines of the European Community and seeks to create the necessary conditions to provide an answer to the "American challenge." But perhaps the most important aspect of the memorandum is a forceful appeal to public opinion in order to promote greater awareness of the problems involved and to generate broad support by influential elites and the public at large for the objectives and strategies of the EEC Commission, as well as for the European Community system in general.

Difficulties of Implementation

Considering previous experiences in European Community decision-making with respect to forward movements in integration, the full implementation of the EEC Commission's plans and ideas may be quite difficult. It would require the member states to give up important national prerogatives or, at any rate, deep-rooted customs that are founded on concepts of national interest and national security. The notion of European Community development contracts for industries in the field of advanced technology would, without doubt, affect the area of national defense, since in this field it is extremely difficult to separate the civilian sphere from the military sphere. Thus, a very divisive factor would be immediately introduced into any deliberations on this subject. Finally, some of the suggestions of the EEC Commission may require amendments of the European Community treaties. To obtain agreement for these revisions among the member governments may be possible only when a common European interest has been clearly defined and fully accepted by the appropriate national authorities and elites.

The reality of these difficulties became immediately evident when the memorandum was introduced to the Council of

Ministers on April 21, 1970. The French insisted that, in the study of the memorandum, full consideration be given to proposals of their own, which included a preferential computer-buying policy for European Community products, to be introduced immediately by the national administrations, and a coordinated European Community policy concerning large foreign investments in the member states. The Dutch requested that, for the time being, work on the proposed industrial policy not go beyond the preparatory stage and that no further progress be made until countries applying for membership could participate in the deliberations.[94]

Meanwhile, the memorandum will be studied by the European Parliament, the Economic and Social Committee, and the Committee of Permanent Representatives. Therefore, little definitive action may be expected by the Council of Ministers until the end of the year. By that time, the EEC Commission may have submitted to the Council of Ministers a number of concrete recommendations, as well as specific draft directives to the member governments, that, if adopted, would set in motion the implementation of the memorandum.

In summary, the EEC Commission memorandum on a future industrial policy of the European Community could promote transnational business collaboration and advance the process of political integration in the future in several ways. It may well serve as an instrument of exhortation and persuasion aimed at the member governments to speed up the implementation of existing directives on legal and policy harmonization. It may become the basis for new directives that would broaden the scope of harmonization measures and introduce new incentives for transnational collaboration ventures. Finally, and perhaps most importantly, it could be a tool to generate fresh support for the European Community system, values, and procedures by politically powerful elites and by the public at large.

NOTES

1.   These are the major problem areas associated with actions and nonactions of the national governments and the EEC that were identified by Comite Européenne pour le Progre Économique et Social [CEPES], Grenzueberschreitende Unternehmungskooperation in der EWG (Stuttgart: Forkel Verlag, 1968), pp. 62-65, (hereafter cited as CEPES study).

According to the survey of Dutch firms by H. W. de Jong and
M. Alkema, Revue du Marché Commun, No. 109 (January-
February, 1968), p. 157, differences in national fiscal regimes
constitute the second most serious problem in their transnational ventures.

2.   The interviews of the author confirmed the findings
of the CEPES study and de Jong and Alkema, op. cit., in
general, but found concern with differing national policies to
be significant also.

3.   See Werner Feld, The European Common Market and
the World (Englewood Cliffs, N. J.: Prentice-Hall, 1967),
pp. 23-30.

4.   For fuller details, see Werner Feld, "National Economic Interest Groups and Policy Formation in the EEC,"
Political Science Quarterly, LXXXI, 3 (September, 1966),
392-411.

5.   For details, see W. H. Balekjian, Legal Aspects of
Foreign Investment in the European Economic Community
(Manchester: University of Manchester Press, 1967), pp. 46-60.

6.   Journal of Commerce (October 17, 1969).

7.   For additional comments on this difficult problem,
see the report of the Economic Commission of the European
Parliament entitled "Les règles de concurrence et la position
des entreprises Européennes sur le marché communautaire
et dans l'economie mondiale," No. 20.507 (April 10, 1969).
(mimeographed).

8.   See the interesting comments by Michel Dancourt
and Henri Lepage "Obstacles psychologiques (et politiques)
aux concentrations et aux fusions intracommunautaires,"
Revue du Marché Commun, No. 109 (January-February,
1968), pp. 131-42.

9.   Die Zeit (April 14 and 28, 1970).

10.   Agence Europe Bulletin (April 15, 1970).

11.   Personal communication from A. P. Weber, Centre
Universitaire d'Études des Communautés Européennes,

University of Paris, February 11, 1970. No precise data are available for the number of refusals. In important cases as reported in the following pages the press uncovers them; in other cases the prospective partners may prefer to keep their unsuccessful efforts for collaboration hidden from any publicity.

12. International Herald-Tribune (October 5-6, 1968) and Le Monde (October 6-7, 1968 and October 13-14, 1968).

13. Le Monde (October 11, 12, and 25, 1968).

14. International Herald-Tribune (October 12-13, 1968) and Le Monde (October 12, 1968).

15. International Herald-Tribune (October 24, 1968). See also Le Monde (October 24, 1968).

16. Le Monde (October 27-28, 1968).

17. Agence Europe Bulletin (December 24, 1968).

18. Le Monde (February 5, 1969 and May 13, 1969). For an excellent resume of the collaboration attempt and its failure, see Le Monde de l' Économie (February 11, 1969), pp. 1-2.

19. Report of the Commission Regarding the Activities of the Communities 1969 (Brussels-Luxembourg, February 1970), par. 111.

20. Agence Europe Bulletin (March 27, 1969).

21. Ibid. (April 1, 1969, and June 19, 1969).

22. International Herald Tribune (September 12, 1967).

23. Agence Europe Bulletin (February 12, 1970).

24. Ibid. (April 22, 1969).

25. Ibid. (March 5, 1970).

26. These major objectives are suggested by the CEPES study and are, in general, confirmed by the interviews and

conversations of the author, as well as by the findings of de
Jong and Alkema, op. cit., p. 156.

27. Le Monde (March 4, 1969).

28. Agence Europe Bulletin (September 16 and 22, 1969
and October 1 and 17, 1969).

29. Ibid. (September 29, 1969).

30. Ibid. (April 21, 1969).

31. Ibid. (January 16, 1969, and May 27, 1969). See
also the report of the Economic Commission of the European
Parliament, "Les règles de concurrence et la position des
enterprises européennes sur le marché communautaire et
dans l'économie mondiale," op. cit., pp. 49-53, which
analyzes the options open for fiscal harmonization;
European Document No. 519, in Agence Europe Bulletin
(March 24, 1969): and K. Peter Mailander, "Mergers and
Acquisitions in the EEC," Journal of International Law and
Politics (NYU), I, 1 (April, 1968), 19-36. For a compre-
hensive discussion of this problem, see the reports by
Joseph Kauffman and Gerard Hutchings, Revue de Marché
Commun, No. 109 (January-February, 1968), pp. 449-74.

32. Agence Europe Bulletin (May 7, 1969).

33. Ibid. (January 13, 1970, February 13 and 20, 1970,
and April 10, 1970).

34. Journal of Commerce (October 6, 1969).

35. Agence Europe Bulletin (September 30, 1969).

36. Ibid. (March 3 and 5, 1969). For details of the
planned conventions, see ibid. (February 12, 1969). For a
discussion of a related problem, the harmonization of trade-
mark laws, see H. W. Wertheimer, "The Principle of
Territoriality in the Trademark Law of the Common Market
Countries," The International and Comparative Law Quarterly
(July, 1967), pp. 630-62. For the latest developments, see
Journal of Commerce (February 10, 1970).

37. For additional information, see Mailander, op. cit.,
pp. 22-26, and CEPES study, pp. 191-95.

38.   See Le Monde (December 6 and 7, 1968); Der Spiegel (October, 1968), pp. 46-70; and Heinz O. Vetter, "Mitbestimmung ist Fortschritt," Europaeische Gemein-schaft (September, 1968), pp. 5-7.

39.   For details, see Agence Europe Bulletin (March 12, 1970).

40.   Journal Official, No. C75 (July 29, 1968).   See also the Report of the Commission Regarding the Activities of the Communities, 1968, pars. 22-33.

41.   For an analysis of pertinent EEC Commission decisions, see Michel Waelbroeck, "Cooperation Agreements and Competition Policy in the EEC," Journal of International Law and Politics (NYU), I, 1 (April, 1968), 5-18; and D. L. McLachlan and D. Swann, Competition Policy in the European Community (London: Oxford University Press, 1967), passim See also Jean Meynaud and Dusan Sidjansky, L 'Europe des affaires (Paris: Payot, 1967), pp. 58-69.

42.   See Agence Europe Bulletin (August 1, 1969).

43.   Ibid.   (February 13, 1969, and July 17, 1969).

44.   European Community (Washington), No. 131 (February, 1970), p. 4; and Agence Europe Bulletin (January 26 and 27, 1970).

45.   Agence Europe Bulletin (February 9, 1970).   See also European Community (Washington), No. 131 (February, 1970), p. 4.

46.   Agence Europe Bulletin (March 5, 1970).

47.   For details, see European Document No. 566, in Agence Europe Bulletin (March 10, 1970).

48.   For details, see European Document No. 565, in Agence Europe Bulletin (March 6, 1970).

49.   Journal of Commerce (February 25, 1970).

50.   For a general discussion of the tactics used by large companies in Europe and their capacity to influence

government and European Community decisions, see Meynaud
and Sidjansky, op. cit., pp. 129-204; and Feld, "National
Economic Interest Groups and Policy Formation in the EEC."

51. Agence Europe Bulletin (October 21, 1969).

52. Ibid. (February 1, 1969).

53. Meynaud and Sidjansky, op. cit., p. 143.

54. See Bela Balassa, The Theory of Economic Integration (Homewood, Ill.: Richard D. Irwin, 1961), pp. 10-14,
21-25, 102-4, 118-34, and 163-67.

55. Ibid., p. 1.

56. John Pinder, "Comecon, An East European Common
Market," paper delivered at the Semaine de Bruges, March
26-29, 1969 (London: PEP, 1969) p. 3. (mimeographed.)

57. Leon N. Lindberg, "The European Community as a
Political System: Notes Toward the Construction of a Model,"
Journal of Common Market Studies, V, 4 (June 5, 1967),
256-57.

58. Ibid., p. 361.

59. Ibid., pp. 360-63.

60. Ibid., p. 371.

61. Ibid., pp. 371-72.

62. See Louis Phlips, "Effets économiques de la
concentration industrielle: Essai d'analyse empirique" (1969)
(Mimeographed.); and H. W. de Jong, "De Concentratiebeweging in de Westeuropese Economie," Economisch-
Statistische Berichten (January 22 and 29, 1969 and February
5 and 12, 1969), especially Table 3.

63. Fortune (August 15, 1969), p. 107.

64. See Le Monde (October 15, 1968).

65. See Frankfurter Allgemeine Zeitung, (April 29, 1969).

66. See Theo M. Loch, "Warten auf ein Wunder, "
Europaeische Gemeinschaft (October, 1969), pp. 4-5; and
Herbert Kriedemann, "Die Gemeinschaft ist in groesster
Bedraengnis, " ibid. , pp. 6-7.

67. Franz-Josef Strauss, "Phrasen schaffen kein
Europa, " ibid. (December, 1968), pp. 3-4.

68. Anthony Downs, Inside Bureaucracy (Boston: Little,
Brown, and Co. , 1969), pp. 84-87. See also Francis E.
Rourke, Bureaucracy, Politics, and Public Policy (Boston:
Little, Brown, and Co. , 1969), pp. 11-28.

69. Max Weber, From Max Weber: Essays in Sociology,
trans. and ed. H. H. Gerth and P. W. Mills (New York:
Oxford University Press, 1958), pp. 228-35.

70. For more information on this intriguing subject,
see Downs, op. cit. , pp. 195-97.

71. See Werner Feld, "The Civil Service of the
European Communities: Legal and Political Aspects, "
Journal of Public Law, XII, 1 (1963), 68-85.

72. Downs, op. cit. , , pp. 242-43.

73. Sueddeutsche Zeitung (June 20, 1969).

74. J. K. De Vree, "Le theme européen dans les
élections générales de 1967 au Pays-Bas" (Europa Institute of
the University of Amsterdam) (Mimeographed.); and Alfred
Jaeger, "Das Thema 'Europa' im Bundestagswahlkampf 1965"
(Forschungsinstitut fuer Politische Wissenschaft und
Europaeische Fragen and der Universitaet zu Koeln).
(Mimeographed.)

75. See Jacques-René Rabier, "The European Idea and
National Public Opinion, " Government and Opposition, II, 3
(April-July, 1969), 443-54, for an excellent analysis of
public-opinion attitudes in the Common Market. See also
Ronald Inglehart, "An End to European Integration, " American
Political Science Review, LXI, 1 (March, 1967), 91-105,
whose optimism regarding the process of integration, based
mainly on attitude surveys of the younger generation, seems
to disregard other, more salient factors.

76. See Le Monde (May 28, 1968) and Le Soir (Brussels) (June 2, 1969).

77. For the latest creations, the Europa Partei and the Parti Socialiste Européen, see Agence Europe Bulletin (May 19, 1969).

78. Ibid.

79. See M. L. Gingembre, "La création d'entreprises à l'echélle européenne: l'avenir des petites et moyennes entreprises." (paper presented at a colloquium held at the Free University of Brussels, October 24-25, 1968). (Mimeographed). The linkage between constituency attitudes and behavior of elected representatives is difficult to evaluate and varies according to different political cultures. For the U.S. experience, see Charles F. Cnudde and Donald J. McCrone, "The Linkage between Constituency Attitudes and Congressional Voting Behavior: A Causal Model," American Political Science Review, LX, 1 (March, 1966), 858-66.

80. See Nicola de Pamphilis, "Azione Sindicale e Concentrazioni Industirali," Conquiste del Lavoro, XXI, 47 (November 18-24, 1968), 7.

81. Agence Europe Bulletin (July 9, 1969).

82. Ibid. (July 25, 1969).

83. Heinz O. Vetter, "The Lessons of the ICFTU Congress, "DGB Report, III, 4 (1969), 38.

84. Agence Europe Bulletin (July 4, 1969).

85. For their programs, see European Document No. 528, in Agence Europe Bulletin (May 30, 1969), and European Document No. 524 in Agence Europe Bulletin (April 29, 1969), respectively.

86. The text of the agreement, Entente pour l' harmonisation de la durée du travail des salariés agricoles permanents occupés dans la culture, can be obtained from COPA. See also European Community (Washington), No. 124 (June, 1969), p. 18.

87.   Ernst B. Haas, The Uniting of Europe (Stanford, Calif.: Stanford University Press, 1968), p. xxxiii.

88.   See International Herald-Tribune (January 17, 1969).

89.   For details, see Agence Europe Bulletin (February 9, 1970).

90.   See ibid. (April 20 and 21, 1970).

91.   See also the rather pessimistic assessment in Frans A. M. Alting von Geusau, Beyond the European Community (Leydon: A. W. Sijthoff, 1969), which is not fully shared by this observer.

92.   Agence Europe Bulletin (March 20, 1970, and April 16, 1970).

93.   See also Philippe Heymann, "Une question de vie ou de mort: une politique industrielle européenne," Communauté Européenne, No. 140 (March, 1970), pp. 25-30.

94.   Agence Europe Bulletin (April 22, 1970).

CHAPTER **4** CONCLUSIONS AND
PROSPECTS

From the foregoing analysis it is clear that, while the
increasing rate of transnational business collaboration in the
Common Market since 1960 has produced a more intensive
degree of economic integration, the effect on political integration, as measured by a rise in the powers of the EEC
institutions, has been slight, producing only small incremental advances. The main effect has been strongly motivated
assistance by collaborating firms and perhaps even leadership for bringing about the initial steps toward fiscal and legal
harmonization. If the harmonization process is permitted to
move forward, the autonomy of the member governments is
likely to be whittled down and larger, incremental advances
in political integration can be expected.

Legal harmonization and perhaps also policy coordination
by the member governments carries with it at least the implicit obligation of no further unilateral changes. As a consequence, the powers of the EEC authorities should be gradually enhanced as the process of harmonization and coordination
progresses. In addition, the development of a European patent
law may result in the assignment of new functions and powers
to the EEC institutions, either de facto or through multilateral
conventions among the member states.

Under the peripheralization-centralization index, a situation would be approached in which the system authorities
cannot overawe but can delimit the activities of subsystem
authorities and keep their own decisions from being overruled.
Under these circumstances, the political activities of an increasing number of political actors would, in all likelihood,
shift toward the central system authorities and, with it, increasing their expectations and perhaps even their loyalties.
This shift may also engender a rise in the European Community support level of politically powerful elites and may enhance the legitimacy of the system authorities as appropriate
political institutions in the eyes of the public of the European
Community. [1]

111

As the conditions for transnational business collaboration improve, as a result of greater fiscal and other harmonization measures and of the eventual disappearance of border control points, the trend toward border-crossing collaboration with the Common Market is apt to receive additional impetus. In turn, the clamor for full implementation of these measures is likely to rise further. Eventually, however, a plateau of satisfactory conditions for transnational collaboration ventures may be reached. At that time, the stimulus of this activity for political integration will cease to operate and the main concern will be the maintenance of the level of integration attained.

Although the incentive for integration growth will have disappeared, however, certain effects--such as the increased legitimacy level of the EEC institutions and procedures and the greater commitment of business and perhaps other elites to European values--would probably persist and would remain influential for possible further progress of political integration in the future. Moreover, the acquisition of vested interests in a certain level of integration would constitute a bulwark against regression or dismantlement of the European Community system and would enhance its stability. If such a sequence of events were to unfold, it would suggest that Professor Paul Reuter's prediction that "it is the industrial leaders who will build Europe"[2] indeed contains a measure of truth, although other potential forces promoting political integration obviously must be considered as well.

It has often been said that an appropriate political will is required to really move Europe toward political unification. Rarely is the term "political will" defined, but it clearly implies an element of leadership. Yet more seems to be needed than a leader. The additional ingredient is the full commitment of the political and administrative elites of the European Community subsystems to the underlying values and procedures of the European Community system. When this happens, political integration is likely to advance in much larger increments.

"THREAT" OF AMERICAN DOMINATION?

It is well known that the strong penchant for European unification that was manifest during the 1950's was generated by the perception of an outside threat--namely, Soviet expansionism toward Western Europe. Could the challenges of the

large American corporations in the EEC and elsewhere be
perceived as a threat that could be instrumental for the resur-
rection of a positive European political will for unification?
In such an event, border-crossing collaboration with Common
Market-wide industrial division of labor might be viewed as
the savior of European independence, and its incremental
value for political integration could increase rapidly.

Some segments of the electronics industry in the Common
Market, such as data-processing and printed circuits, are
increasingly becoming a near monopoly of American firms
and enterprises controlled by Americans. The existing gap
between the capabilities of European firms in this field is
likely to widen rather than to narrow. It is not inconceivable
that purely European firms either have to drop out of the competitive race or have to become mere satellites of American
corporations. Although some EEC-based firms--such as
Philips, Siemens of Germany, and France's Compagnie
Internationale d'Informatique (CII)--are now challenging IBM
and other American firms in the computer field, their experiences and research resources are insufficient to make a dent
in the very large market share commanded by U.S. companies.
(This share is eight times as great as that of the European
firms including Great Britain.) Although some of the European governments consider it a question of honor to have
national computer manufacturers in their countries and support their companies in the assault on the American hegemony,
they are much less generous than the American Government
is when it comes to providing finances for the necessary research. Thus, it does not seem likely that the separate
European companies will be successful in their challenge.[3]

The American companies are not only strong in the
electronics field, but also in other sectors of the European
economies, especially in the "growth" industries. Estimates
of plant and equipment expenditures of affiliates of U.S. corporations in the Common Market for 1970 are close to the
$2 billion mark, nearly double those of 1965 and up more than
$300 million from 1969.[4] Nevertheless, despite the wide-
spread condemnation of American domination of the European
economy and the theoretical acknowledgment of the need for
large, transnational enterprises and collaboration to combat
superior American technology and managerial skill, a threat
to Europe is not perceived with any intensity. One important
reason is that the European Community economies have derived and continue to derive extensive benefits from American
investments. These include the creation of new job

opportunities, often in industrially neglected regions; a valuable contribution to export earnings, with IBM ranking among France's top exporters; and gains in technology and know-how.

The EEC Commission is concerned about the long-run effects of this situation, however, and has established an ad hoc organization that is to survey periodically the comparative standings of the American enterprises in Europe and the exclusively European business organizations within the EEC. Some legal restrictions on American investments in the Common Market have been advocated from time to time, but, even if the EEC Commission were to make appropriate proposals to the Council of Ministers to that effect, it is very doubtful that Germany, the Netherlands, and Belgium would go along, no matter how mild these proposals might be. [5]

For this reason, it also seems unlikely that a French recommendation put forth in March, 1970, will be accepted. [6] According to this proposal, the six Common Market nations should evolve a common position on investments from third countries, which, hopefully, would contain a subtle determination against U.S. interests. (In this connection, a poll conducted in France during February and March, 1970, is interesting. According to this poll, the majority of Frenchmen were in favor of American investments in France. Only one person in four declared that American investments in France were positively harmful to French interests, although the proportion rose to one in three among farmers and one in two among members of the Communist Party. The strongest support came from people in the 20-34 age group and from industrial executives and members of the liberal professions.

The EEC Commission memorandum of April, 1970, clear rejects a defensive strategy that would erect barriers against the investment of third countries or the activities of American firms or others in the Common Market. On the contrary, the EEC Commission advocates an offensive strategy consisting of measures, including transnational collaboration, to enable European firms to become capable of facing what is usually called the "American challenge."

BRITISH COLLABORATIONS WITH
COMMON MARKET FIRMS

As pointed out in Chapter 2, the number of British collaborations with EEC firms compares very favorably with those between Common Market enterprises. In fact, with respect to production subsidiaries and financial participations, British companies showed a considerably higher degree of initiative than did their EEC counterparts. Does this high level of transnational activity have any implications for British entry into the Common Market, which has continued to be the avowed goal of the British Government since 1961?

The basic motivations for collaboration agreements concluded between British and EEC firms are economic and have been stimulated by the desire to hurdle the external tariff barriers of the European Community and to exploit the opportunities flowing from the establishment of the large single market.[8] It is interesting to note that, as Tables 2 and 3 indicate, from 1967 to 1968 the total number of marketing and production subsidiaries, as well as financial participations, set up or sponsored respectively by British firms in the Common Market almost quadrupled. This increase does not appear to be due to any concerted strategy of British industry or the government, but it is likely to be the result of the complete elimination of all tariff barriers inside the EEC, considered to be the point of no return for the movement toward full economic integration.

From seventy-four interviews conducted by Charles de Hoghton with senior executives of British firms engaged in some kind of transnational collaboration with Common Market enterprises, it is apparent that socio-psychological problems, conceptual differences regarding business methods, and divergencies in goals and expectations encountered in intra-EEC collaborations were also found in British-EEC joint ventures. Nonetheless, although some of the partnerships went sour and failed, in the majority of cases the difficulties were overcome or the problems were reduced to manageable proportions. In fact, half of the respondents stated that the scope of their agreements had widened since their conclusion to cover a broader range of products or activities. Others said that the relationship had become closer.[9]

Since the mechanics of collaboration and coordination of these joint efforts are apt to be similar to those of the intra-EEC ventures, the same transactional flows between the staffs of the collaborating firms, including those of a human and social nature, are likely to be created. Thus, the conditions are set for political socialization processes to become operative, which should lead to a gradual adoption of European values and beliefs among the collaborating staffs. This, in turn, may have some favorable implications for the

entry of Britain into the Common Market and, perhaps, for
eventual progress toward political integration. It would be
imprudent, however, to attribute too much importance to
British-EEC business collaboration as a promotional device
for speeding up Britain's admission to membership in the
Common Market, particularly since the number of British
firms involved in ventures with EEC companies has remained
relatively small.

   The same considerations that apply to the effects of transnational business collaboration in the EEC on the progress of
political integration hold true mutatis mutandis. Certain
groups pursuing protectionist and nationalistic goals and,
perhaps, civil servants fearful of losing their position of
power are seeking to prevent Britain's entry into the Common
Market. Moreover, a variety of additional elements, such as
agriculture and maybe defense, are likely to play more influential roles regarding the success of the accession negotiations than are the wishes of the business community.

   It is a problem of agriculture and, in particular, of the
high fixed prices of farm commodities under the European
Community's CAP that has cooled the earlier fervor of the
British to enter the Common Market. The prospective increase in the cost of living in Great Britain resulting from
Common Market membership has been largely responsible
for increasing opposition to EEC membership on the part of
public opinion. (In October, 1969, an opinion survey in
Britain showed that only 22 per cent of the respondents were
in favor of entry, whereas 54 per cent were opposed.)

   Nevertheless, an overwhelming majority of the members
of the powerful Confederation of British Industry (CBI) have
retained their strong support for Britain's membership. This
stance has reinforced the efforts of the CBI leadership to urge
the government to push ahead with the negotiations. The CBI
leadership, however, has also indicated that safeguards for
the British economy must be bargained out before a final
agreement can be reached. [10] Thus, the views of the CBI
reinforce whatever effects transnational business collaboratio
between British and EEC firms may have with respect to
British membership in the EEC.

   The final decision on British membership, of course, is
up to the British Government, which in February, 1970, issue
a White Paper addressing itself to "The United Kingdom and
the European Communities: An Economic Assessment."
Emphasizing that the British position, including the balance-
of-payments, was now better than it had been in previous
years, it made the following significant declaration:

The economy of the United Kingdom is stronger, the
Six are now unanimously in favour of our entry, and
the political arguments for closer unity between
Britain and the other countries of western Europe
have also become stronger. The major uncertain
factor still is the balance of economic advantage
particularly in the short run. . . . [This] demon-
strates the need for negotiations to determine the
conditions on which the opportunity for entry could
be seized. Failure to reach agreement in these
negotiations would not necessarily condemn Britain
or the European Communities to political or economic sterility. But Europe would have lost another
historic opportunity to develop its full economic po-
tentialities in the interests of the welfare and
security of its citizens . . . [11]

Although the White Paper confirmed that the increase in food
costs necessitated by the high fixed market prices of the CAP
could well result in a rise of between 4 per cent and 5 per
cent in the cost of living in Britain, it also expressed hope
that by joining the EEC the United Kingdom would achieve a
much higher growth rate for its GNP, since its industry could
benefit from a market of nearly 300 million inhabitants, and
that, therefore, the gamble could clearly pay off in the long run.
    Once Britain has joined the Common Market, the impetus
for British firms to collaborate with companies of the six EEC
nations is likely to be enhanced, especially when tax harmonization has made further progress and a European patent agreement has been achieved. A decision, for instance, to set up
a manufacturing unit jointly with a company in another EEC
country would not be determined any longer by tariff considerations, however, but by the degree to which such a move
will contribute to production rationalization, will improve the
physical marketing of the product within the Common Market,
and will enhance its export opportunities to third countries.
After British entry, the contribution of the growing interlacement between British enterprises and firms of the former
member countries to the process of political integration will
most likely not differ much from that made earlier by border-
crossing collaboration among the six present members.

LESSONS FOR POLITICAL
INTEGRATION THEORY

The question was raised in Chapter 1 of the relationship between the processes of economic and political integration. Of particular interest here is whether the two processes can be seen as separate points on a continuum, ending up in political unification of an international region. A basically affirmative view of this question has been central to the doctrine of functionalism, to which a majority of American political scientists seem to be committed; however, various reservations to this proposition have been voiced over the last few years, even by adherents of functionalist theories.

Automaticity of Political Integration

The fundamental premise of functionalism is that particular functions in the sphere of economic and social welfare can become the subject of international cooperation as areas of mutual interests and needs are recognized. For the satisfaction of the interests and needs involved, functionalists, committed to pragmatism and gradualism, hope for a piecemeal transfer of governmental authority from national to international institutions.[12] When member states of a regional international organization such as the EEC are engaged in an economic integration scheme, it is contended that the logic of functionalism can lead to the phenomenon of "spillover." In his conceptualization of neofunctional hypotheses, Philippe C. Schmitter defines spillover

> as the process whereby members of an integration scheme--agreed on some collective goal for a variety of motives but unequally satisfied with their attainment of these goals--attempt to resolve their dissatisfaction either by resorting to collaboration in another, related sector (expanding the scope of the mutual commitment) or by intensifying their commitment to the original sector (increasing the level of mutual commitment) or both.[13]

Consequently, collective action in policy sectors not contemplated in the original integration scheme may well lead to an added delegation of authority to the central regional

institutions. The question debated increasingly since the
late 1960's is how potent the spillover process is in shifting
governmental authority from the national to the central institutions and whether the process will automatically result
in the transformation of a "politically inspired common
market to an economic union, and finally to a political union
among states."[14] Haas, who with many other functionalists
fully espoused the automaticity of this transformation, in the
past, now recognizes its limitations. He has acknowledged,
as previously noted, that a political process built and projected from pragmatic interests, as is the functional process,
is inherently weak and is susceptible to reversal, especially
when opposed by important elites whose reasons for opposition
may be buttressed by ideological commitments.[15] (See pp.
94-95, above.)

For Schmitter, the potential for the automaticity of the
transformation process continued to be high, although it depends on whether the members of an integration scheme score
"high" on a variety of variables relating to the background of
the countries participating in the economic integration scheme,
to the conditions existing during the initiation of this scheme,
and to factors that manifest themselves during the process en-
suing after the schemes become operative.[16] According to
Schmitter, automaticity refers to "a (theoretically) high
probability that spillover . . . will occur, " but he stresses
that the term does not imply "linearity" or "evenness" in the
integrative process. Rather, it implies that "conflict between
national actors is very likely to be forthcoming but that it is
likely to be resolved by expanding the scope or level of central
institutions. While there is no guarantee they will always be
successful, the manipulation of such crises by regional actors
lies at the core of the integrative dynamic."[17] According to
Schmitter, neofunctional logic emphasizes for this purpose
"the role of bureaucratic practice, organizational ideology,
and the creative interventions of administrative and political
elites."[18]

The neofunctionalists contend that the transformation
process from a common market to a political union is aided
by "politization." This term refers initially to an increase in
the controversiality of joint decision-making, which, in turn,
is likely to lead to a widening of the audience or clientele
interested and active in integration. Schmitter argues that
"somewhere along the line a manifest re-definition of mutual
objectives will probably occur, " which he calls "transcendence"
and which "may or may not involve a definitive, self-confessed

shift from formerly economic to manifestly political goals . . .
In any case, the new goals involve an upward shift in either
scope or level of commitment and, ultimately, there will be
a shift in actor expectations and loyalty toward the new regiona
center. This shift may be neither overt nor exclusive; rather,
"in all likelihood, it will involve a new 'larger' allegiance
superimposed, rather than replacing, existing national loyalties. "[19]

Critics of Functional Hypotheses

Since the late 1960's the hypotheses of the functionalists
and the neofunctionalists have encountered increasing opposition as it became obvious that the process of political integration in the EEC not only was failing to move forward, but,
on the contrary, seemed to regress. In contrast to the logic
of functional integration, Stanley Hoffmann has posited the
"logic of diversity. " The latter stresses the freedom of
action insisted upon by the national governments, which re-
stricts the domain in which the logic of functional integration
operates to that of welfare. In fact, even in that domain,
issues may become infected by the disharmony that reigns in
other areas, especially those of key importance to the national
interest--namely, foreign policy and defense. These are the
areas of "high" politics, as distinguished from welfare, or
"low, " politics.[20] Hoffmann argues that intra-EEC relations
have become subordinated to the divergencies of the member
governments about the outside world and that the European
Community has become a stake in the rivalry of its members
about the international system as a whole.[21]

Other critics of functional theories with respect to the
transformation of regional systems include Karl Kaiser, who
contends that these theories do not lend themselves easily for
application to the EEC's external relations, particularly when
issues of "high" and "low" politics become intermingled. He
considers these theories as partial approaches to the study
of regional integration and proposes a broad empirical system
analysis approach toward the international system as a whole,
within which sector integration or functional integration can
be researched as part of the manifestations of system change.

Lawrence B. Krause argues that "political integration
will occur only as a result of positive political decision to brin

it about, not as a result of economic pressures alone." Although economic integration requires coordination of many
economic policies that involve essentially political decisions,
Krause holds that formal political institutions may not be
needed to bring about this coordination. "A 'hidden hand'
toward policy coordination is directed by the market mechanism and it has proven to be very effective in the EEC."[23]

Finally, Roger D. Hansen suggests that three factors have
led to an overestimation of the expansiveness of functional integration in the European Community:

> They were, first, a failure to relate the process of
> regional integration closely enough to relevant inter-
> national system factors; second, a tendency to deny
> rather than to investigate the continuity between high
> and welfare politics . . .; and third, a failure to recog-
> nize that sizeable (and equitably distributed) economic
> gains would result from a common market coordinated
> by sovereign states rather than managed by cease-
> lessly expanding supranational authorities.[24]

Although some of the criticism against the theories of
functionalism with respect to regional integration seems valid,
this study of transnational business collaboration with the Common Market illustrates the continuing potential force of functionalism for the transformation of a regional system. This
process is likely to be extremely slow, however, and there
may well be flaws in the neofunctionalist hypotheses.

Events have proven Hoffmann right; that is, as interests
become involved in the integration process that are perceived
by the national governments to be of national importance,
resistance to giving up sovereign prerogatives rises sharply.
And Kaiser is correct in stating that issues intertwined in
both welfare (low) and high politics make it especially difficult for the logic of functionalism to exert its potency. But
it is precisely in the area of EEC external relations that,
since 1969, progress is being slowly made toward a transfer
of authority from national to central institutions, inasmuch as
the EEC Commission is given an expanded role in the formu-
lation and execution of commercial policies toward third
countries.[25] This seems to bear out Hansen's contention that
a continuity indeed exists between low and high politics, which
needs further investigation in the future.

Lessons from Study

Although Krause is correct that the "hidden hand" of the
market mechanism is indeed a powerful force for the coordination of economic policies among the member states--indeed,
it is a major condition for the operation of the logic of
functionalism--it is doubtful that this coordination can be
assured on a long-term basis without central political institutions. A measure of stability and predictability regarding
these policies is essential to sustain the dynamics of the
market mechanism in a regional unit. These elements may
not be present when one has to depend solely on the good will
of the national governments, subject to a variety of political
pressures; therefore, central institutions appear to be a
necessity.

The Benelux countries have had a customs union since
1944, but fiscal harmonization, common economic policies,
and uniform border regulations and practices have not been
developed through the "hidden hand" of the market mechanism,
despite the fact that, since 1944, three treaties between the
member countries have sought to bring about an "economic
union," which is usually characterized by the harmonization
of economic policies. To move ahead with this objective, the
governments of the three countries found it necessary in
spring, 1969, to set up an Office of Incentive, a clear indica-
tion of the need for central institutions, which so far have
been lacking in the Benelux union.[26]

As Hansen states, sizeable and equitably distributed
economic gains could result from a common market coordinated by the sovereign states. But, considering the pressures
of national groups and the difficulty of determining without bias
exactly what is "equitable," it seems that central institutions
can perform the task of coordination to the satisfaction of all
concerned much better than the national governments can. In
fact, this enables the national authorities to place the onus
for "equitable" distribution of economic gains on the shoulders
of the central authorities when national groups argue, in fact,
for "inequitable" distribution.

One of the major flaws of the neofunctionalist hypotheses,
however, is the great reliance placed on bureaucratic practice and the ability of the European Community or any other
regional bureaucracy to move the political integration process
forward. Undoubtedly, the expertise of European Community
officials with respect to the economic affairs of the EEC is
generally superior to that found in the national administrations,

and this may be a significant advantage when it comes to pro-
posing the right kind of decision against a set of deadlines
and using the technique of package deals that safeguard the
collective economic welfare of the member states. It is also
possible that these circumstances engender, at times, political
decisions that are perhaps produced rather by "indirection,
almost by guile, " as Haas and Schmitter put it, [27] than by a
straightforward approach.

But, despite the fact that politization, an important condition for the operation of the spillover process according to
Schmitter, had set in as the result of the increased controversiality of the regional decision-making process in the
1960's, the European Community officials have been able to
capitalize on this situation only to a limited degree during the
latter part of that decade. One reason may have been that the
purposeful ambiguity necessary for the "strategy of indirection"
may, in fact, have aroused the determined opposition of the
national administrations and the fears of the national bureaucracies that their positions of power might be undermined
through the "conspiratorial schemes" of the European Community civil service. Another reason may be that, as a consequence of the generally adverse political conditions prevailing in the EEC since 1963 for the progress of political
unification, many European Community officials have lost
much of their formerly strong ideological fervor for European
unity and that, because of the reverses suffered, they have
confined themselves to the purely technical functions of their
jobs.

This study suggests that the national bureaucracy of the
member states is one of the essential factors for the success
or failure of the spillover process, and, therefore, its attitudes, beliefs, and norms of conduct should become the focus
for intense research. A close look at the national bureaucracies is likely to yield new insights into the decision-making
style within the European Community system, as well as into
the adaptability of national governments, [28] and national
bureaucratic behavior may therefore emerge as an important
variable in the comparative study of regional integration.

A strategy of the European Community's central leadership that would encompass a compensatory scheme for the
national bureaucracies in the member states, as advocated
earlier (See pp. 88-91, above.), may produce greater results in advancing political integration than might reliance on
a strategy of "indirection" on the part of the European Community civil service, which may be resented and therefore be

self-defeating. "Creative interventions of administrative
elites," which, according to Schmitter, provide impetus to
the spillover process, are not likely to emanate from the national bureaucracies to any degree unless a compensatory
scheme provides the necessary inducement.

Although, as Schmitter points out, politization is apt to
lead to a widening of the clientele interested and active in
integration, this study raises some doubts that political elites
in the member states will engage in "creative interventions"
to a meaningful degree to push the spillover process forward.
The role that the elected political elites may play in this respect must be seen in the context of their objective to be
victorious in national and local elections and in this the issue
of political integration generally plays a very small part.
Although some of the statesmen in the member states may be
sincerely in favor of moving political integration toward a
united Europe, the interests of most political elites in support
of this movement seem to be marginal at best at present,
despite declarations of many politicians to the contrary.[29]

It is also interesting to note that the formerly high prestige accompanying the election of a national deputy to the
European Parliament has been declining in recent years.
Therefore, such elections are not sought any more with the
same alacrity as in earlier years, the quality of the European
parliamentarians has suffered, and their ability to influence
their colleagues in the national legislatures has been reduced.
Under these circumstances, the creation of a positive political
will to bring about unification, as suggested by Krause, seems
to be almost impossible.

Sincere commitment of support for the European Community system on the part of the political elites would be the first
step toward the creation of such a will, but such a commitment
is likely to depend again on the individual's perception of its
need for a successful election. As incremental advances are
made slowly and haltingly in the political integration process,
as a result of transnational business collaboration and other
forces, and as issues from this process become more con-
troversial for national electoral processes, this need may in
due time be perceived to an increasing degree. Again, this
is an area where much additional empirical research has to
be done for a more meaningful comparative study of regional
integration and for a better understanding of which variables
are crucial for the process of integration.

The widening of the audience or clientele interested and
active in integration as the result of increased politization

must also not be overestimated in terms of strengthening
transnational (European) interest groups and their activities.
The main transmission belts for demands and services used
by various groups in the Common Market countries remain
those connected with the national administrations and political
parties, and they continue to handle an enormous amount of
economic and social demands and services with a huge
bureaucracy. The national bureaucracies, in turn, are
pleased with this situation and will, as has been seen, make
every effort to retain their clientele.

Finally, this study seems to indicate that the neofunctionalists may have given too little weight to the phenomenon of
social integration and its relationship to political integration.
Social integration, as defined by Joseph S. Nye, involves "the
creation of a transnational society . . . or the abolition of
national impediments to the free flow of transactions."[30]
Clearly, the transactional and communication flows in the
social and human realms activated by transnational business
collaboration between the staffs of participating enterprises
fall under this definition of social integration; as has been
suggested, this flow has an effect on political integration by
raising the saliency of the issue area under study. Again,
additional research into the transnational linkages between
certain elites and segments of the national publics may be
fruitful in shedding further light on their connection to the
process of political integration.[31] (Nye distinguishes between
mass social integration and the social integration of special
groups or elites. For the former, he uses as indicators of
progress the amount of trade, mail, telephone calls, etc.
For the latter, the determination of indicators is much more
difficult.)

Although this study concurs with Stanley Hoffmann's view
that, considering the Common Market as an incipient political
system, the authority of its institutions remain limited, its
structures are weak, and its popular base is restricted and
distant;[32] its outlook for the future is not pessimistic. If
nothing else could be gleaned from this study, a very slow
transformation of the system can be detected. Of course, a
determined struggle to resist this transformation can be fore-
seen, and in all likelihood long periods of stagnation will occur.
But the logic and forces of functionalism still appear to be
operative and slow and halting progress, measured perhaps
in decades rather than years, seems likely to be made.

Although it may well be true, as Pierre Pescatore argues,
that the significance of an economic union may not lie in the

possibility of political unification but in the ability of the member states to preserve their political autonomy through the
formation of a large, viable market, [33] increasing constraints
flowing from the operation of transnational and international
forces may induce politically powerful elites to perceive some
form of unification as advantageous, provided the interests of
these elites can be reasonably safeguarded. Thus, if the
necessary leadership should be available, the appropriate
political will may be created to move ahead with unification.
In the meantime, much more empirical research is needed
to identify and circumscribe the variables underlying the
process of political integration. Although current efforts to
refine the measurements of presently accepted variables are
to be commended, the continuous search for the critical
variables--all of which have not been discovered--is equally
essential. [34]

SUMMARY

The following seven theses may be useful in summarizing
some of the findings of this study.

(1) The prospects of successful transnational business
collaboration ventures are greater if the partners are of
approximately equal size. These prospects are smaller the
more the expectations of the partners differ as to the results
of the collaboration, the greater their emphasis on their
traditional conceptions of doing business, and the more serious
the inability of their management personnel to surmount the
language barrier. The more pronounced the latter three conditions, the stronger is the inducement for national collaborations or mergers.

(2) The closer the net of transnational business collaboration, the greater is the likelihood of incremental progress
toward political integration, but full acceleration of the political integration process depends on the degree of support
for the European Community system tendered by politically
powerful elites.

(3) The greater the harmonization of fiscal and other
pertinent laws in the EEC member states and the closer the
coordination of their economic policies, the stronger is likely
to be the trend toward transnational business collaboration
and the higher the prospects that such collaboration will be
successful.

(4)   The greater the involvement of management and technical personnel in transnational business collaboration ventures, the more the likelihood exists of the development of a
"Europe"-oriented elite that through cross communications
with other elites could solicit added support for the European
Community system and that may constitute an energizing and
stabilizing force for political integration.

(5)   Although transnational business collaboration may be
perceived as a threat by labor unions, it has also spurred
them to clamor for transnational bargaining in order to "level
up" benefits for labor in different countries, eventually including wages.   The greater their success in these endeavors,
the higher is likely to be their interest in supporting transnational business collaboration and the European Community
system.

(6)   The more national administrative elites perceive
their positions as vested interests and supranational decision-
making as a threat to their positions of power, the less likely
will be the harmonization of pertinent laws and the coordination
of economic policies in the EEC member states.

(7)   As long as the question of "Europe" does not arouse
sufficient interest among the electorates of the EEC member
states to affect significantly the outcome of the elections of
elected political elites, these elites will not be motivated to
provide energetic support to the European Community system
and their statements in favor of a united Europe must be
judged mainly as lip service.

NOTES

1.   Legitimacy involves the capacity of a system to engender and maintain the belief that the existing political
institutions are the most appropriate ones for the society.
Legitimacy is evaluative; groups regard a political system
as legitimate or illegitimate according to the way in which
its values fit with theirs.   See Seymour M. Lipset, Political
Man (Garden City, N.Y.: Doubleday and Co., 1960), p. 77.

2.   Quoted in André Marchal, "Necessité économique
des fusions et concentrations intracommunautaires," Revue
du Marché Commun, No. 109 (January-February, 1968), p.
44.   A similar function was performed by business interests
in the United States and Switzerland.   Charles A. Beard points

out that support for the adoption of the U.S. Constitution came
principally from the cities and the regions where the commercial, financial, and manufacturing interests were concentrated. These interests had been adversely affected by the
system of government under the Articles of Confederation and
they therefore sought to secure greater protection through a
"revision" of the articles that culminated in the present constitution. See Charles A. Beard, Economic Origins of Jeffer-
sonian Democracy (New York: MacMillan, 1915), p. 464; and
his An Economic Interpretation of the Constitution of the United
States (New York: MacMillan, 1960), p. 63 et passim. For
the Swiss experience in 1815, see Charlotte Muret, "The Swiss
Pattern for a Federated Europe," in International Political
Communities, An Anthology (Garden City, N.Y.: Doubleday
and Co., 1966), pp. 149-73.

    3. For more information on this subject, including
statistical data, see Philip Siekman, "Now It's the European
Versus IBM," Fortune (August 15, 1969), pp. 86 ff.

    4. U.S. Department of Commerce, Survey of Current
Business, XLIX, 9 (September, 1969), 20. For a more ex-
tensive survey of American investments in Europe, see
Christopher Layton, Trans-Atlantic Investments (Boulogne-
sur-Seine: The Atlantic Institute, 1966); and especially Rainer
Hellmann, Amerika auf dem Europamarkt (Baden-Baden:
Nomos Verlagsgesellschaft, 1966).

    5. Agence Europe Bulletin (September 22, 1969).

    6. Ibid. (March 20, 1970).

    7. Journal of Commerce (March 10, 1970).

    8. Charles de Hoghton, Cross-Channel Collaboration
(London: Political and Economic Planning, n.d.), pp. 8-10.

    9. Ibid., pp. 20-43.

    10. See Journal of Commerce (April 30, 1970).

    11. The Times (February 11, 1970).

    12. See David Mitrany, A Working Peace System (London
and New York: Royal Institute of International Affairs, 1966).

13.   Philippe C. Schmitter, "Three Neo-Functional Hypotheses About International Integration, " International Organization, XXIII, 1 (Winter, 1969), 162.

14.   Ernst B. Haas, "The Uniting of Europe and the Uniting of Latin America, " Journal of Common Market Studies, V, 4 (June, 1967), 327.

15.   Ibid., pp. 327-33.

16.   For details regarding background, initiation, and process variables, see Ernst B. Haas and Philippe C. Schmitter, "Economic and Differential Patterns of Political Integration: Projections about Unity in Latin America, " International Organization, XVIII, 4 (Autumn, 1964), 711-19.

17.   Schmitter, op. cit., p. 164.

18.   Ibid.

19.   Ibid., p. 166.

20.   Stanley Hoffmann, "Obstinate or Obsolete? The Fate of the Nation-State and the Case of Western Europe, " Daedalus, XCV, 3 (Summer, 1966), 882.

21.   Ibid., p. 865

22.   Karl Kaiser, "The U. S. and EEC in the Atlantic System: The Problem of Theory, " Journal of Common Market Studies, V, 4 (June, 1967), 394 and 410.

23.   Lawrence B. Krause, European Economic Integration and the United States (Washington, D. C.: The Brookings Institution, 1967), p. 24.

24.   Roger D. Hansen, "Regional Integration, Reflections on a Decade of Theoretical Efforts, " World Politics, XXI, 2 (January, 1969), 256. See also Edward L. Morse, "The Politics of Independence, " International Organization, XXIII, 2 (Spring, 1969), 311-26.

25.   Agence Europe Bulletin (October 13, 1969).

26.   Ibid. (April 29, 1969).

27.   Haas and Schmitter, op. cit., p. 717.

28.   See ibid, pp. 716-17. For the measurements of different variables of the integration process, see Mario Barrera and Ernst B. Haas, "The Operationalization of Some Variables Related to Regional Integration," International Organization, XXIII, 1 (Winter, 1969), 150-60; and Philippe C. Schmitter, "Further Notes on Operationalizing Some Variables Related to Regional Integration," International Organization, XXIII, 2 (Spring, 1969), 327-36.

29.   See, in this connection, Robert Weissberg, "Nationalism, Integration, and French and German Elites," International Organization, XXXIII, 2 (Spring, 1969), 337-47.

30.   Joseph N. Nye, "Comparative Regional Integration: Concept and Measurement," International Organization, XXII, 4 (Autumn, 1968), 863.

31.   See also the work done by Carl J. Friedrich, especially as editor of Politische Dimensionen der Europaeischen Gemeinschaftsbildung (Koeln: Westdeutscher Verlag, 1968); and by Karl Deutsch, especially "Communication Theory and Political Integration" and "Transaction Flows as Indicators of Political Cohesion," in The Integration of Political Communities, ed. Philip E. Jacob and James V. Toscano (Philadelphia: J. B. Lippincott, 1964), pp. 46-97.

32.   Hoffmann, op. cit., p. 885.

33.   Pierre Pescatore, "La notion du marché commun dans les traités instituant l'Union économique belgo-luxembourgoise, le Benelux et les communautés européennes," in En hommage à Victor Gothot (Liege, Faculté de droit, 1962), pp. 497-546.

34.   For analyses of presently accepted variables, see Barrera and Haas, op. cit.; and Schmitter, "Further Notes on Operationalizing Some Variables Related to Regional Integration."

SELECTED BIBLIOGRAPHY

SELECTED BIBLIOGRAPHY

Almond, Gabriel A., and Verba, Sidney. Civic Culture.
Boston: Little, Brown and Co., 1965.

Alting von Geusau, Frans A. M. Beyond the European Community. Leyden: A. W. Sijthoff, 1969.

Balassa, Bela. The Theory of Economic Integration. Homewood, Ill.: Richard D. Irwin, 1961.

Balekjian, W. H. Legal Aspects of Foreign Investment in the
European Economic Community. Manchester: University
of Manchester Press, 1967.

Barrera, Mario, and Haas, Ernest B. "The Operationalization of Some Variables Related to Regional Integration,"
International Organization, XXIII, 1 (Winter, 1969),
150-60.

Behrman, Jack N. "Multinational Corporations, Transnational
Interests and National Sovereignty," Columbia Journal of
World Business, IV, 2 (March-April, 1969).

Comité Européen pour le Progrès Économique et Social.
Grenzueberschreitende Unternehmungskooperation in der
EWG. Stuttgart: Forkel Verlag, 1968.

Dawson, Richard E., and Prewitt, Kenneth. Political Socialization. Boston: Little, Brown and Co., 1969.

de Hoghton, Charles. Cross-Channel Collaboration. London:
Political and Economic Planning, n.d.

de Jong, H. W. "De Concentratiebeweging in de Westeuropese
Economie," Economisch-Statistische Berichten (January
22 and 29, 1969, and February 5 and 12, 1969).

_____. "Spécialisation, concentrations et Marché
Commun," Revue de l'Économie du Centre-Est, X, 40
(April-June, 1968).

Dell, Sidney. A Latin American Common Market? New York: Oxford University Press, 1966.

de Pamphilis, Nicola. "Azione Sindicale e Concentrazioni Industriali," Conquiste del Lavoro, XXI, 47 (November 18-24, 1968), 7.

Deutsch, Karl. "Communication Theory and Political Integration," The Integration of Political Communities. Edited by Philip E. Jacob and James V. Toscano. Philadelphia: J. B. Lippincott, 1964.

_____. "Transaction Flows as Indicators of Political Cohesion," The Integration of Political Communities. Edited by Philip E. Jacob and James V. Toscano. Philadelphia: J. B. Lippincott, 1964.

De Vree, J. K. "Le thème européen dans les élections générales de 1967 au pays-bas." Europa Institute of the University of Amsterdam. Mimeographed.

Downs, Anthony. Inside Bureaucracy. Boston: Little, Brown and Co., 1969.

Drancourt, Michel, and Lepage, Henri. "Obstacles psychologiques (et politiques) aux concentrations et aux fusions intracommunautaires," Revue du Marché Commun, No. 109 (January-February, 1968).

Dreyer, H. Peter. "EEC Key to European Mergers," Journal of Commerce (March 8, 1966).

Easton, David. A System Analysis of Political Life. New York: John Wiley and Sons, 1965.

European Economic Community Commission internal document, published in U.S. Congress, Senate, Committee on the Judiciary, Hearings on Economic Concentration, before the Subcommittee on Antitrust and Monopoly of the Committee on the Judiciary, Senate, on S. Res. 233, 90th Cong., 2d sess., 1969, part 7A.

Feld, Werner. "The Civil Service of the European Communities: Legal and Political Aspects," Journal of Public Law, XII, 1 (1963).

_____. The European Common Market and the
World. Englewood Cliffs, N. J.: Prentice-Hall, 1967.

_____. "National Economic Interest Groups and
Policy Formation in the EEC," Political Science Quarterly, LXXXI, 3 (September, 1966).

Friedman, Wolfgang G., and Kalmanoff, George. Joint International Business Ventures. New York: Columbia University Press, 1961.

Friedrich, Carl J., ed. Politische Dimensionen der Europaeischen Gemeinschaftsbildung. Koeln: Westdeutscher
Verlag, 1968.

Gingembre, M. L. "La création d'entreprises à l'echelle
européenne: l'avenir des petites et moyennes entreprises."
Paper presented at a colloquium held at the Free University of Brussels, October 24-25, 1968. Mimeographed.

Goldmark, Francis M. "Europe Catches the Merger Fever,"
Columbia Journal of World Business, IV, 2 (March-April,
1969).

Haas, Ernst B. The Uniting of Europe. Stanford, Calif.:
Stanford University Press, 1968.

_____. "The Uniting of Europe and the Uniting of
Latin America," Journal of Common Market Studies, V,
4 (June, 1967), 315-343.

_____, and Schmitter, Philippe C. "Economic and
Differential Patterns of Political Integration: Projections
about Unity in Latin America," International Organization,
XVIII, 4 (Autumn, 1964), 705-37.

Hellmann, Rainer. Amerika auf dem Europamarkt. Baden-
Baden: Nomos Verlagsgesellschaft, 1966.

Heymann, Philippe. "Une question de vie ou de mort: une
politique industrielle européenne," Communauté Européenne, No. 140 (March, 1970), pp. 25-30.

Hoffmann, Stanley. "Obstinate or Obsolete? The Fate of the
Nation-State and the Case of Western Europe," Daedalus,
XCV, 3 (Summer, 1966), 862-915.

Inglehart, Ronald. "An End to European Integration, " American
Political Science Review, LXI, 1 (March, 1967).

Jaeger, Alfred. "Das Thema 'Europa' im Bundestagswahlkampf
1965." Forschungsinstitut fuer Politische Wissenschaft
und Europaeische Fragen an der Universitaet zu Koeln.
Mimeographed.

Jurgensen, Harald, and Berg, Hartmut. Konzentration und
Wettbewerb im Gemeinsamen Markt-Das Beispiel der
Automobilindustrie. Goettingen: Vandenhoeck and Rup-
recht, 1968.

Kolde, Endel J. International Business Enterprise. Englewood Cliffs, N. J.: Prentice-Hall, 1968.

Kriedemann, Herbert. "Die Gemeinschaft ist in groesster
Bedraengnis, " Europaeische Gemeinschaft (October, 1969).

Layton, Christopher. European Advanced Technology--A Programme for Integration. London: George Allen and Unwin,
1969.

_____. Trans-Atlantic Investments. Boulogne-sur-
Seine: The Atlantic Institute, 1966.

_____. "Trois idées pour une stratégie indus-
trielle, " Communauté Européenne, No. 139 (February,
1970).

Lecourt, Robert. "Concentrations et fusions d'entreprises,
facteurs d'intégration européenne, " Revue du Marché
Commun, No. 109 (January-February, 1968).

Lindberg, Leon N. "The European Community as a Political
System: Notes Toward the Construction of a Model, "
Journal of Common Market Studies, V, 4 (June, 1967).

_____. The Political Dynamics of European Eco-
nomic Integration. Stanford, Calif.: Stanford University
Press, 1963.

Lipset, Seymour M., Political Man. Garden City, N. Y.:
Doubleday and Co., 1960.

Loch, Theo M. "Warten auf ein Wunder," Europaeische
    Gemeinschaft (October, 1969).

McLachlan, D. L. , and Swann, D. Competition Policy in the
    European Community. London: Oxford University Press,
    1967.

Mailander, K. Peter. "Mergers and Acquisitions in the EEC,"
    Journal of International Law and Politics (NYU), I, 1 (April,
    1968).

Marchal, André. "Necessité économique des fusions et con-
    centrations intracommunautaires," Revue du Marché
    Commun, No. 109 (January-February, 1968).

Meynaud, Jean, and Sidjansky, Dusan. L'Europe des affaires.
    Paris: Payot, 1967.

Meynen, Johannes; Friedmann, Wolfgang; and Weg, Kenneth.
    Columbia Journal of World Business, I, 2 (Spring, 1966).

Mitrany, David. A Working Peace System. London and New
    York: Royal Institute of International Affairs, 1966.

Morse, Edward L. "The Politics of Independence," Inter-
    national Organization, XXIII, 2 (Spring, 1969), 311-26.

Muret, Charlotte. "The Swiss Pattern for a Federated Europe,"
    in International Political Communities, An Anthology.
    Garden City, N. Y. : Doubleday and Co. , 1966.

Phlips, Louis. "Effets économiques de la concentration in-
    dustrièlle: essai d'analyse empirique." 1969. Mimeo-
    graphed.

Pinder, John. "Comecon, An East European Common Market."
    Paper delivered at the Semaine de Bruges, March 26-29,
    1969. London: PEP, 1969. Mimeographed.

Rabier, Jacques-Réné. "The European Idea and National
    Public Opinion," Government and Opposition, II, 3 (April-
    July, 1969).

Rourke, Francis E. Bureaucracy, Politics, and Public Policy.
    Boston: Little, Brown and Co. , 1969.

Saclé, Robert. Revue du Marché Commun, No. 109 (January-February, 1968).

Schmitter, Philippe C. "Further Notes on Operationalizing Some Variables Related to Regional Integration," International Organization, XXIII, 2 (Spring, 1969), 327-36.

Siekman, Philip. "Now It's the European Versus IBM," Fortune (August 15, 1969), pp. 86 ff.

Stonehill, Arthur, and Nathanson, Leonard. "Capital Budgeting and the Multinational Corporation," California Management Review, X, 4 (Summer, 1968).

Strauss, Franz-Josef. "Phrasen schaffen kein Europa," Europaeische Gemeinschaft (December, 1968).

Tabatoni, Pierre. "Remarques sur les obstacles psycho-sociologiques à la coopération internationale," Revue du Marché Commun, No. 109 (January-February, 1968).

Tinbergen, Jan. International Economic Integration. 2d rev. ed. Amsterdam: Elsevier, 1965.

Toulemon, Robert. Agence Europe Bulletin. March 20, 1970.

U. S. Department of Commerce. Survey of Current Business, XLIV, 9 (September, 1969).

Vernon, Raymond. "Economic Sovereignty at Bay," Foreign Affairs. XLVII, 1 (October, 1968).

_____. "Multinational Enterprise and National Sovereignty," Harvard Business Review (March-April, 1967).

Vetter, Heinz O. "The Lessons of the ICFTU Congress," DGB Report, III, 4 (1969), 38.

_____. "Mitbestimmung ist Fortschritt," Europaeische Gemeinschaft (September, 1968).

Waelbroeck, Michel. "Cooperation Agreements and Competition Policy in the EEC," Journal of International Law and Politics (NYU), I, 1 (April, 1968).

Weber, A. P. "Concentrations en Europe," Direction, No.
    160 (April, 1969).

_____. "Les mouvements de concentration en
    Europe et la pénétration industrièlle et commerciale,"
    Direction, No. 148 (March, 1968).

Weber, Max. From Max Weber: Essays in Sociology. Trans-
    lated and Edited by H. H. Gerth and P. W. Mills. New
    York: Oxford University Press, 1958.

Wertheimer, H. W. "The Principle of Territoriality in the
    Trademark Law of the Common Market Countries," The
    International and Comparative Law Quarterly (July, 1967).

ABOUT THE AUTHOR

Werner J. Feld, Professor of Political Science and Chairman of the Department of Political Science at Louisiana State
University in New Orleans, has been a close student of European integration since 1960. He is the author of The European
Common Market and the World (1967) and The Court of the
European Communities: New Dimension in International Ad-
judication (1964). In addition, he has published a number of
articles on various aspects of the European Community.

Professor Feld received a degree in law from the Univer-
sity of Berlin and a Ph.D. in political science from Tulane
University. He was Fulbright Professor at the College of
Europe during the academic year 1968-69 and was Visiting
Professor at Johns Hopkins University in Bologna.